T0354870

SECRETS ON ACCELERATING YOUR GROWTH

52 WEEKS OF SKILLS AND PRINCIPLES FOR GROWING YOUR SMALL BUSINESS

ALEX DAVYDOV

authorHOUSE

AuthorHouse™
1663 Liberty Drive
Bloomington, IN 47403
www.authorhouse.com
Phone: 1 (800) 839-8640

Published by AuthorHouse   12/10/2019

ISBN: 978-1-7283-3599-5 (sc)
ISBN: 978-1-7283-3600-8 (e)

Print information available on the last page.

This book is printed on acid-free paper.

CONTENTS

MONTH FOUR
GETTING LEADS IN THE DOOR

MONTH FIVE
CUSTOMER RETENTION

MONTH SIX
BUILD YOUR NETWORK

MONTH SEVEN
STAY UP TO SPEED

MONTH EIGHT
TIME & FINANCES MANAGEMENT

DEDICATION

This book is dedicated to my mother-in-law, Maggie Gavlaev.

In business, positive attitude and demeanor drive not only attention, but attraction. A positive environment in the workplace not only keeps a strong bond between the staff, but creates a feeling of belonging for clients. Maggie had that special ability to bring light to everyone surrounding her. She owned a hair salon, and every time I would pass by to say hi, the entire salon was full of energy, smiles, laughter, which made me want to spend more time there. Around Maggie, everyone wore a smile. During our family functions, she was the light of the gathering. She would tell us stories, sing songs and motivate the positive and homey feel, which kept the bond among the family always strong. At all the parties and wedding celebrations, she would be the first one to light the hall with her dancing and her wide smile motivated and brought all the guests together on the dance floor. Unfortunately, she left us in 2013, but her daughter (my wife) Yaffa Gavlaev, has taken over to keep that light always shining bright at what was Maggie's Hair Design, and is now known as Style Glam Salon (www.styleglamsalon. com). Memories of Maggie still light up people's days with the delight of her warm presence.

PREFACE

My mother-in-law is a hairstylist with her own salon. She didn't have marketing or advertising of any kind, other than the `open' sign on the door. As soon as we implemented an appointment booking system, she increased sales. Taking that one small step in her business model made a difference.

90% of small business owners are just like my mother-in-law, they have many strong entrepreneurial skills, but they haven't modernized their business, or fully adopted all the skills necessary for growing their business. They have a skill to share, or a passion for their product, but they don't know how to operate a business and make it grow. I wrote this book to educate small business owners on how to properly run a business so that they aren't just breaking even, but actually profiting. I designed this book so that they build the skills and gather the tools to truly accelerate the growth of their business.

Most businesses just sit and wait, they don't do any exposure. These small business owners open a shop, but don't get the word out about their business. They think just turning on the open sign is enough, but the business never crosses people's radar, or they're never given a reason to go in.

But if people know the basics of running a business, then their business will become extremely profitable. Any business has the potential to be a million-dollar business, if you have the basics on how to run a business.

So, I wrote this book to educate small business owners to give them the basics for running their business. I spend a lot of time learning. But not just learning, I implement the knowledge. Everything that

I've learned how to implement I've included in this book. It comes from my experience as an active learner.

I also wrote this book to leave a legacy, leave something behind with my name on it that shares my experiences and what I've learned so that others can benefit. In the future, my kids will read this book, and whether they have a business, they will be able to experience some of my story.

INTRODUCTION

'Knowledge is potential. Action is Power.'

–Mark Russo

What do business owners want?
They want to grow, to be profitable.

If you really want your business to grow without you spending thousands of dollars on different (often unnecessary) material and without making mistakes or missing key facets, this book is for you. I'm all for hiring coaches and taking classes and reading books. They teach you one thing about business, but they don't teach you the basics of *operating* a business. About not only onboarding clients, but also retention. They just give you a broad idea, not the meat and potatoes.

My fifteen years of business experience—to include hundreds of books, videos, podcasts, and dozens of courses—are distilled into this book that will teach you how to operate—and grow—a small business.

For as long as I can remember, I wanted to be a business owner. With the help of my dad and family, I was able to borrow money and open a business. My dad always owned a business. My grandfather had his own business. Almost all my family members always had their own businesses. Growing up in that kind of family instilled in me those values, ethic, and dreams. It gave me the courage to open up my own business at 22 years old.

My family left Uzbekistan when I was 12 years old. We fled Uzbekistan for racial reasons. I knew I was Jewish, but we weren't strict adherents, but because of that title, because people knew we were Jews, in a Muslim country. My brothers and I would always get into fights, all of the other kids saw us as enemies, just because of that title. Most of the Jews fled Uzbekistan, including us. We came to the U.S., to have some freedom and light. I'm glad we did so because now we all have opportunities to actually become someone.

When we first moved here, my father went from a successful small business owner, a watchmaker, to struggling to make ends meet. During my childhood and teenage years in the United States, I watched my father try at all kinds of jobs after giving up his watchmaking business in Uzbekistan. Finally, though, he opened up a watchmaking shop in New York, and was able to find success and happiness yet again.

Watching my father make so many sacrifices, try and fail, and try and fail, then finally find success, instilled in me the value that knowledge is potential, and action is power.

A lot of things won't work, but it'll never work if you never try. I can't just have my money sit under the pillow and do nothing. I'd rather lose it than have it under my pillow. I'd rather try to succeed and have that money make me more money. We have to keep re-investing our money to become more successful. My big dream is to one day have the ability to build a multi-family 50-100 unit apartment building. I love building, I love the idea of having my creative stamp on family homes for hundreds of people. Everything I do with my companies is geared toward my long-term dream. Every risk I take is worth it, for its own sake, but also because it moves me toward my dream.

A lot of people know a lot of information. That information is potential. Potential for them to be great, successful.

Action is power. Without the action, the application, then the information becomes useless.

When they implement that knowledge, it becomes power. Any action causes a reaction. Whether it works or fails, it becomes power. When you take an action, things change. Even when it doesn't work the first time, you have still taken that first step, that first action toward your goals.

It is with that in mind that I structured the information in this book to not just be potential—information that enters your brain—but to inspire and guide you toward action.

How to use and read this book

This book covers the meat and potatoes of operating a small business in the modern era. I teach you how to use your time wisely, how to efficiently modernize your business for the information age, how to create and run successful marketing campaigns, how to develop your staff, and how to grow your customer base. Each month takes you through information and practical steps for you to take right away to help you improve your reach and grow the number of people who are excited and happy to spend money at your business.

The book is designed to break down all of the concepts and principles of operating a small business into actionable steps for you to take. The first 10 months are structured as daily reading and daily action steps for you to take based on the new information. The best way to use the book is to do the daily reading and block out time for the 15-60 minutes worth of work each day.

Each month focuses on a different facet of business operation. Each month builds different skills, based on the topic. But there are some common threads throughout the whole book, some skills that you will grow week by week and month by month.

The first and main skill is self-reflection. When you take action, when you implement knowledge, you need to stop and think about how it went, so that your next action will be even better. Each month has several self-reflection activities. You'll be amazed at how pausing to reflect, to analyze, observe and digest makes you more efficient at operating your business. When you stop and think about what you are doing, and why you are doing it, all kinds of insights and new ideas will spark.

The second main skill is time and project management. This skill is broken down into smaller components that build upon each other throughout the course of the book.

Most business owners want their freedom, they want free time. But they do everything themselves and are in their businesses day in and day out. What most business owners want is more time to themselves.

I was working 24/7. My family is very close and we all live in the same city. I was working so much that I was missing out on family events and time with my cousins and siblings. It was so bad that I even almost missed my own sister's wedding because I had to teach a class. I thought to myself, why am I running my own business if it means I keep missing out on things that are so important to me? I went out and learned what I needed to learn so that I'd never miss out on family like that again.

This book teaches you how to free up time.

The first step is understanding what you need the time for. If you don't know what you need the time for, then you'll have all the time and not know what to do with it. Knowing I wanted my time for my family inspired and motivated me to learn what I needed to learn about business operation to have free time.

As I learned new things about business operations, I started to take time off. That time off grew from one day, to two, until I was regularly taking three-four days off at a stretch. I began to have a lot of free time on my hands with the changes I was making in my business.

If you have too much time on your hand it messes with your mental and emotional well-being. Too much unpurposed time can be as detrimental as too little. So you need to understand what this extra time will be used for.

Have other goals: a 2nd business, traveling, family, hobbies, some blend. If you open up free time but don't have anything for it, it will enervate you, you'll become bored and restless, and probably end up going right back to your old behavior of pouring yourself into your business at the expense of a full dimensional life.

You think that nobody else can do what you do. Yes, you can't replicate yourself, but you can make someone somewhat like you, but you free up your time to do more important things, and that is well, well worth it in the long run, both for personal and professional reasons.

So, take some time now to start reflecting on what it is you want to free up time for. Let it marinate, let yourself dream big. If you don't dream big, you'll never come even close to achieving those big things.

The third skill that gets built across the entire book is having an open mind, a learner mindset. When you're willing to try new things, to fail, to get back up and try again, when you're willing to learn from whoever will teach you, no matter how uncomfortable it is, you can't help but succeed. Many of the business owners I work with are pretty uncomfortable with making changes, so this is a real skill, to have an open mind to learning. I designed the book to make learning and implementing new information as simple and easy as possible. By the time you get to the end of the book, if you do the work, if you plan your time, take action, reflect, and have a goal for your free time, you will be amazed at the results.

Remember, Try hard to be first. Try hard not to be last, if you're not last, you're winning.

MONTH ONE
HEALTHY BODY = HEALTHY BUSINESS

I'm a health fanatic. I'm at the gym every day, often twice a day. From my years of owning a business and interacting with other business owners, there's no getting around it. If you're not healthy, your business will suffer 100%.

Month One. Time to face the facts. No more putting off all your good intentions to eat better, sleep better, exercise more. If you want to accelerate your business, it's time to commit to your health.

There are many different models for what health looks like. The Army has its performance triad of sleep, activity, nutrition, which I think is one of the most straightforward ways to approach your health. Are you getting enough sleep, and restful sleep at that? Are you getting regular physical activity that gets the blood circulating, heart pumping, and muscles exerting? And, are you putting things into your body that make it feel energized, or are you putting things in that make you lethargic and foggy-headed?

We start business acceleration with physical health because a healthy body has a direct impact on mental and emotional health. In other words, when you feel physically healthy, you are more confident, and think more clearly, among other effects.

It's easy to think up new intentions. It requires discipline to carefully select the right intentions and follow through in a realistic and disciplined manner. Practicing the discipline of caring for your health will help prepare you for the discipline of making changes and improvements to other aspects of your business, and you'll begin to feel the reward almost immediately in your nervous system, digestive system, and energy levels in general.

The simple truth is, it all comes down to you deciding to change your priorities.

Change your priorities to expanding your lifespan, having more self-confidence, and earning more respect from employees? Why wouldn't you do that?

Well, we live in a country with an obesity problem, a pandemic of sleeplessness, and a billion dollar industry of pills. So, changing priorities is something that is going to take some dedicated effort on your part. This month, we break it down and make it easy to get some momentum going on prioritizing your health.

WEEK 1
LET'S GET ACTIVE

Monday: Why Your Physical Health Matters

Physical health improves your mental and emotional health. When your body is cared for you have more energy, and more mobility. It increases your self-confidence. It expands your lifespan. Staying physically healthy means you have a deep reservoir of resources to draw on to help you run your business.

It's one thing to hear, it's another to know it intellectually, and then it's another to have truly absorbed this idea into your life. Absorption requires self-reflection (an essential skill for anyone, triply so for a business owner). Self-reflection is a skill you are going to be using a lot of through the rest of these chapters. We start practicing the art of self-reflection with caring for your health because it is the easiest way to learn this art, and when you get to the challenging stuff all the benefits of caring for yourself will accelerate your ability to master the other skills.

Self-Reflection Exercise

Take a moment to sit and relax. Maybe walk outside, maybe find somewhere peaceful that the space itself starts to help you relax. Bring this book and a pen with you.

After a minute or two of relaxing and letting your surroundings absorb your attention, start to think about your body. Listen to it. What parts of your body have something to say? If you haven't been taking care of your body, you'll probably be hearing a lot of complaints. Don't tune

3

them out. Don't judge them or yourself. Your first inclination is going to be judgment. Notice the judgment and let it go.

Take a few moments to observe your breath. Keep drawing your attention back to it as your mind wanders.

After following your breath for a few moments, ask yourself, why is it important to me to take care of my physical health?

Record whatever pops into your mind.

If you don't have a personal, meaningful *why* to take care of your body, all the statistics and motivational speeches in the world won't do much. All the willpower and good intentions in the world won't do much. Remember, knowledge is potential.

Getting in touch with that deep inner personal space, listening to it, and then acting is the only way change happens.

Consider how you can revise your why to put it somewhere you'll see every day. Your revision should be creative and inspiring in a way that is unique to you. I have a picture of a chess game in my office, and every time I look at it, it inspires and motivates me to consider my role as the visionary of my business. My picture reminds me that I am the game, and that re-sets my mind and motivation to be better in the ways that I am working on to improve as part of accelerating my business.

Your personal daily visual reminder can gradually become more unique and complex as you practice and grow throughout the year ahead [and beyond!]. If a post-it note in your bathroom is going to work, go that route. If you want to sketch something out, or create a bookmark, or find an image online, or ask a friend to make you something—it's your call. What is important is to put it in a place you will look at every day to get that boost and reminder of what you are working for.

A visual reminder of your 'why' that you let catch your eye and mind every day—even for 10 seconds—can have a powerful impact on your ability to stay the course toward your goals.

Brainstorm ideas in your journal. Make it a priority to create a visual and give it a home today. You can always go back and create another one later. Let's focus on getting the ball rollin' here in this first week of the first month of you accelerating your business.

Tuesday: When to Exercise

The easiest time to work out is first thing in the morning, especially for beginners or people who haven't worked out in a long time. If you are a beginner, it's time to get started. Set your alarm clock for 5 minutes earlier tomorrow—don't put it off, do it right now. If your alarm clock is at home, set a reminder to ping when you get home tonight, and when you hear it go off, get 'er done. Putting it off only compounds the issue.

Tomorrow morning when your alarm goes off 5 minutes earlier, do whatever is easiest. Maybe for you that is stretching, maybe it's walking up and down all the stairs in your house for 5 minutes, maybe it's some jumping jacks or push-ups. Whatever you commit to, do it. Right now we are just building the habit of getting up and working out in the morning. You can increase your work-out effort once you've built the muscle of getting up and getting your heart pumping and your muscles moving.

Even if you already have a workout routine, I want you to do this exercise of 5 minutes of movement first thing. Giving the body a little bit of time to warm up the circulation system first thing in the morning has proven benefits. (It can also help you break any nasty little habits of looking at a screen first thing).

Remember, this week is all about getting the ball rolling and learning how to take manageable chunks of change. In other words, this week we are building reps on 2 of the most important skills of business acceleration.

We talk about accountability and failure, the skills that nurture keeping the ball rolling and taking on manageable chunks of change in chapter 12. If you want to skip ahead and give it a glance through, go for it. If you're at capacity, own it and don't take on too much by the extra reading.

After your 5-minute work-out tomorrow, jot down how you feel right after in the notebook you started yesterday.

Then, jot down how you feel after lunch. See if you can notice any minute differences from having worked out in your body. If you like, and it suits your style, you can keep a daily journal of observations post-workout and post-lunch. It really only takes about 30 seconds to record and can be a huge game-changer in the long run. But, again, if you've already got a manageable chunk of change just getting up 5 minutes earlier, be honest and own that. This book is designed so that you can re-read it multiple times and continue to benefit. Maybe next year is the right time to record exercise effects on the body. Maybe 3 months from now. Maybe never. Own your self-reflection; own what manageable means to you.

For those of you with established work-out routines, what has been on your mind to explore in terms of taking care of your physical body to the next level? Can you come up with a 5 minute activity that you can start to build into your day?

Wednesday: Accountability

One of the first questions I always get when talking about the importance of your health to the health of your business is how to stay motivated. Monday we practiced a visualization technique for maintaining motivation. Yesterday built on that with beginning to practice using self-reflection to determine what a manageable chunk of change is without losing momentum on that ball continuing to roll. Today we talk about the 3rd technique for keeping momentum on your system of care for your health: an accountability partner.

Honestly, my first recommendation is to hire someone. They will train you on technique, they will work you harder than you will work yourself, and they will help you reach your goals.

Yes, a trainer is a financial investment. Remember, though, you are investing in the length and quality of your life—your joints as you age, your memory, your ability to take care of yourself, your ability to continue to run your business. When you think about the ROI of investing in a personal trainer, it's hard to understand how the money isn't worth it.

Don't just pick any trainer. Take the time to make sure that they have the qualifications to train you: are they fit? Do they have a good diet? Do they have a personality/coaching style that meshes with your learning style? Do they have a solid plan for keeping you accountable?

Now, if you have some solid knowledge on how to take care of your body, maybe you don't need to invest in a trainer. Maybe investing in a gym, or some exercise classes is a better fit. But you are still going to want to create the conditions where people hold you accountable for whether or not you work out.

The best way to do it is to find someone with a similar goal, and to set up a way to help each other stay on track. You might use rewards, or turn it into a mini competition, if those tools work for you. Maybe it's enough for you to just ask a spouse, family member, or close friend to ask you once a week how your work-out plan is going and have them help you troubleshoot.

Remember, you are asking your circle for their time and care, which means you have to respect it by doing your highest-caliber effort to stick to the plan you set for yourself (without forgetting to be flexible and humble to how your plan needs to change as new data comes in).

And, finally, maybe you are the kind of person where you can keep yourself accountable for your work-out goals. Maybe you can create a spreadsheet, or reminders on your phone or computer, set yourself a goal (and maybe a reward), and then achieve that goal.

Be realistic. Where are you in your relationship to exercise? Which of these options makes the most sense for you to reach your physical health goals? Take 10 minutes to begin getting that set up. Research trainers or ask around. Figure out who in your network might be a good work-out buddy. Get your plan rolling with 10 minutes of your time right now. Use your journal to jot down notes before choosing and implementing your course of action. 10 minutes is manageable, right?

Thursday: Types of Exercise

There are dozens of different ways you can give your body the physical workout it needs to stay fit and powered up to give you a great day at work and at home.

You need to pick something that you enjoy, that gives you a full-body workout.

Some options include a YouTube search for 'full body workout.' Or use Google to find pdfs of work-out routines.

Learn a martial art, or take up dancing, yoga, kick-boxing, etc. You don't need to take a class to do the workout at home, although at the class you will learn the proper technique and be challenged. You can learn technique from the internet, as well, although nothing beats person-to-person learning when it comes to taking care of your body.

But for right now, the priority is to just get moving. You know when you are sweating or not; you know when your heart is pumping; you know when your muscles feel the ache of effort. Investing in learning from others is a huge help, but my main priority for the beginners out there is to just build the habit. You can refine as you go along. So, pick something that engages with you, and start adding it to your 5 minutes every morning. Maybe you mix it up, maybe Mondays, Wednesdays, and Fridays, are stairs and jumping jacks, and Tuesdays and Thursdays is a 10-minute exercise video you find online.

Take 10 minutes and plan out what your morning routine is going to be. If you do evening classes or training sessions, you are still going to want to stick to the morning workout—things always come up in the evening, and if you stay with the morning workout, your efforts to take care of your physical health are way less likely to get derailed by the chaos of life.

Write out your plan in your journal.

Friday: Keep the Momentum Moving Forward

I'm lucky. I started physical activity with my brothers in elementary school, and physical activity became one of my passions in high school. I'm lucky to have had the momentum on keeping physically active started at such a young age. If you're not much of one for getting your body moving, or you do some physical activity, but you haven't continued to up your game on your physical health, then you have months, years, maybe even decades, of momentum going the opposite direction to overcome.

That's why my emphasis this week has been so strongly on the concepts and principles of manageable chunks of change. Taking on the momentum of your habits with your physical body builds the skill up before we turn it to more abstract (and more challenging) types of change that are so necessary to accelerate your business.

Take some time over the weekend to self-reflect about what thoughts or patterns of thoughts show up for you that encourage or justify avoiding working out. See if you can take an objective stance toward those thoughts, just observe them at first. Maybe write them down in the space below. And then return to them in a couple weeks to see if you can have a new attitude toward the thoughts that impede your ability to keep the momentum moving forward on taking charge of your physical health.

WEEK 2
DIET

Monday: What's Your Motivation for Eating Better?

In my mid-20s, I went to the doctor for a checkup. The doctor told me I had high cholesterol, and that I needed to work out more. Well, at the time I was a wrestler and a martial artist going to competitions; I was training very hard. I said, "there's no more I can do, I'm an athlete."

His response: either you work out more or you change your diet.

So, even if you are the best of the best at exercising, you still need to pay attention to what you put into your body that gets transformed into energy and tissue. As a business owner, you are already well-aware of how input creates output. The same principle applies with food. We all know it, we all know the saying, you are what you eat. But, as we talked about last week, knowing it intellectually is different than knowing it at that deeper level (action is power).

Flip back to last Monday, go through the same reflection exercise, this time, instead of focusing on your whole body, see if you can focus on your stomach and digestive system.

Write your why in your journal. Pin it somewhere in your kitchen that you will see every day.

Tuesday: Quit Snacking

Your digestive tract is like a washing machine. When you are washing clothes, you don't stop the washer every 15 minutes to add more dirty clothes—the clothes you pull out at the end would not be clean. It's the same with your gut. When you snack all day, your digestive tract doesn't have time to finish the previous load before starting the next one. This creates an unnecessary tax on your resources.

One of the easiest things you can do to quickly feel more energy is to cut down on snacking. (Though it will take at least a couple weeks to re-train your blood sugar to not crash out without the snack infusions of sugar into your blood stream).

Self-Reflection Exercise

Write down your snacking habits. What do you snack on and what for? Is it for the crunch, the salt, the sweet, or?

Where do you get the snack foods from? Are they on your desk, in a vending machine, in your fridge at the end of the day?

Now that we've gathered the data, we can start to make a plan. The best way to help yourself out is to change the location of your snack foods, and to be aware of when you are feeling cravings, and what you are feeling cravings for.

So, let's start with making the snack foods not hold a prominent space. Give them away, throw them out, put them in the bottom of the hardest to access kitchen pantry. Do it today. If you are going to keep them around, keep them out of sight, and make it so you have to work a little to get to them. If you go to vending machines, try to make a habit of removing your one dollar bills either before you get to work, or putting them away in a desk drawer when you get to work.

We've created a bit of a pause in your mental/emotional process of reaching for that snack food, so let's take the next step. If you know you always have a snack around 10:30am, you know your body, mind, and emotions are going to be primed to have that snack at that time and are going to protest when the expectation of the habit isn't met.

How can you be ready for that? Can you replace it with another habit? What is it that is feeding the habit? Boredom? Stress? Low energy? If it's boredom or stress, try adding a little physical exercise when that food craving hits. If it's low energy, drink some water and remind yourself that your energy levels will go up once you kick snacking to the curb.

If you haven't moved your snack food, do that now. Once the food is in its new home, take some time to think about what motivates you to snack, and come up with a plan for how you are going to be ready when your body or your boredom or your stress get upset when their regular attention paid to them via food doesn't happen.

Remember, your plan can change as you test out what does and does not work. Manageable chunks of change is what we are looking for.

Wednesday: Incorporate New Recipes

In this busy modern world, it is easy to eat out, or to cook the same few recipes over and over. Quite often, cooking at the end of the day takes mental and physical resources that just aren't there.

Food is as much emotional comfort as it is anything else. Making changes to comforting routines when you are dealing day in and day out with the stress of running a business can be challenging. It's easy to justify putting off eating healthy when those fast, hot, cheesy foods are so convenient and so emotionally satisfying.

But, it is a short-term satisfaction that leads to long-term pain.

There are many ways to tackle the process of beginning to improve your diet. When you eat out, you can eat less of your favorite food and more veggies/salads. You can meal prep on the weekend, you can invest in a nutritionist or another program that helps take off the load of meal prep. You can find accountability partners and start up some kind of community effort (i.e., trading off cooking, potlucks, etc).

You are going to want to take the same lesson from snacking about investigating why you are eating what you are eating. *Are you eating out of habit? Emotion? Physical addiction to sugar or processed flour? Take the time to get outside or somewhere peaceful. Don't skimp the work of self-reflection.*

You can also make slight changes to the recipes that you currently have on rotation.

But, what is really going to help is doing your research, and finding recipes that hit that sweet spot of enjoyable, are simple enough to master quickly, and help you get the nutrients you need.

Thursday: Hydrate

> **"If the human body is a machine, then water is the oil that keeps it running."**
> –UFH Health Podcast

Are you drinking enough water? Water helps lubricate your joints, your organs and lungs, and helps your muscles work smoothly. Making sure you are hydrated is as important, if not more, than what you eat. It takes a lot of careful effort to be able to undo old habits and learn to discern thirst from hunger.

It can help to hydrate your system to begin the day drinking 12-16 ounces of water first thing out of bed. It's better to drink warm water, but that takes some getting used to (warm water requires less effort by your system to ingest). This gets water to your body, and it helps you orient to making sure you get enough water throughout the day.

The other main technique is to carry a water bottle. Just like with moving the snack foods out of prime real estate, moving water *into* prime real estate can help you drink enough to keep your body running smoothly.

Take a few minutes to create your plan for staying hydrated, and take whatever first, easy steps you can to get that habit down.

Friday: Listen to Your Doctor

When I went to the doctor and found out I had high cholesterol, I didn't ask for a pill. I listened to what my doctor told me I needed to do to address the problem. I did a lot of research, and I made the effort to change my diet. Now, my cholesterol levels are fine, and people regularly mistake me as being 10 years younger than I actually am.

What happened? I listened to my doctor.

So, when you go in and get your check-up, and they explain what is starting to get off-kilter inside your body, you need to listen. You can do more research, experiment with different approaches to addressing the issue, but at the end of the day, you have to take a problem-solving mindset, rather than just letting the problem go, or taking a pill to mask the symptoms.

When you last went to the doctor, what did they say? Is there something in their check-up that you ignored? Take a few minutes to write about it, self-reflect on why you might've done that, and come up with a plan to begin to address what your doctor told you.

Or, you can do some research and consult with a nutritionist or other type of health-care provider that you trust to provide sound feedback and insight that you can listen to and incorporate into your lifestyle.

WEEK 3
EXERCISE YOUR MIND

Monday: Why it matters

Now that you've got your physical health on track, it is time to turn to health habits for your mind.

One of the biggest problems I see in working with business owners is that they are unwilling to learn. They aren't willing to try new things, they don't want to admit that a different process could be better. Mental health means your ability to focus, your ability to remember, your ability to see a situation clearly, and your ability to be creative and come up with clutch insights into the challenges that face your business.

Take a few moments to reflect on the last time you got frustrated or upset with someone. I mean really upset. What thoughts went through your head? Write them in your journal.

Look over what you wrote. Can you take a step back from the heat of your anger and see the situation from their perspective? Can you think of something you didn't consider, or that they were right about? If it is hard for you to separate from your anger and take a balanced perspective, or if you don't often think about how you can improve your approach to a problem— be it interpersonal or otherwise—then **your business needs you to learn to exercise and open your mind as much as it needs you to take care of your physical health**.

15

Tuesday: A Learning Habit

Keep your memory honed, your ability to focus sharp, and your capacity to receive new information in peak shape with a regular research routine. It doesn't have to be burdensomely time-intensive. But learning should be a regular part of your week. That's another reason why I set the book up this way, to help you build that capacity.

Learn because your curiosity is piqued, not because it's another thing to check off the to-do list. Listen to different points of view or perspectives, as that helps you keep an open mind, which as I said yesterday is an essential element to running a growing small business.

So, what subjects grab your interest? As a business owner, you want to be absorbing business material as well as what subjects grab you. Ideally, this is a blend of books and articles, podcasts and classes. Books are meatier and have valuable information that articles simply can't accomplish, but articles are segments of information that are digestible and well-suited to these modern times. And classes give tons of amazing information, in a format designed to help full understanding.

It's not enough to just let words pass your eyes or ears, so pause to consider their meaning through reflection.

If you don't have a learning habit, can you carve out 3 20-minute segments of time that you can focus on reading? That is a good place to start. Remember to balance curiosity with the needs to cultivate open-mindedness and to learn what you need to learn to improve the operations of your business.

Open your calendar and see where you have 3 blocks of 20 minutes where you can fully focus on what you are reading.

Wednesday: The Power of Self-Reflection

Self-reflection is what keeps you honest. It helps you fully and truly realize whether or not you are moving closer to your goals, whether or not your goals are truly valuable, and helps you realize what was or was not a mistake. Self- reflection is troubleshooting at the most profound level. As a small business owner, just as your physical health affects your business, so does your ability to admit mistakes and learn from them, as we began to discuss on Monday of this week.

Self-reflection is a key skill of this book. All of the following chapters ask you to use your ability to self-reflect. Go back to the first day in this month and look over the exercise for tuning into your body. How easy was that exercise for you? Did it take some effort to get calm? Did you cut corners, skimp, notice you didn't fully understand one of the directions but breezed through it any way?

Those questions are self-reflective. For the purposes of this book, there are two extremes you can fall into—obsessively thinking you can do better, and lazily thinking it's all fine and who cares or notices if you cut that corner. You can fall into either extreme, or a blend of the two. Take a few moments to go through the breathing exercise and see what thoughts pop into your mind about your ability to self-reflect.

Record those insights in your journal.

Thursday: Unwind Your Mind & Give It Quality Down Time

In this day and age, with an inundation of information and sensory experience, it is probably more important to cultivate healthy unwinding time than any other part of taking care of your mind covered so far. Quality down time for your mind is what gives all the previous material the oil to keep running.

If you binge watch TV on a regular basis, or you drink a little too much a little too often, that is a sign that your mind is not getting the quality unwinding time that it needs.

The best ways to unwind your mind are nature, quality time with loved ones in the evening, indulgent-yet-healthful rituals such as massages, bubble baths, etc, and exercise. If your mind is wound tight, this is going to be more challenging in some ways than taking care of your body, because your body will never lie to you about what it wants, but your mind will lie on a regular basis if it feels justified.

Self-Reflection Exercise

Describe what you do right when you get home from work.

Describe what you do in the 20 minutes before bed.

Looking over the data you've gathered, what do you observe? Is it quality unwind time or not? Simple question, straightforward answer.

Take a few moments to create a plan for making a small change to how you unwind right after work, and how you unwind right before you go to bed.

Friday: Putting It All Together

So, from this week we began to learn that taking care of your mind is supported by taking care of your physical health, nourished by letting your curiosity lead you to filling your mind with new information, sustained by the ability to self-respect and by quality unwind time.

It's easy to veer between extremes, to start up a new habit, drop it, and back and forth. And some of this is just the natural rhythm of being human. But as a small business owner, your ability to take charge of your focus, energy, and direction is essential to long-term growth and success.

Look back over the past 3 weeks. How well is incorporating manageable chunks of change to your physical health going? How is including more reading going? How do you see the unwind and self-reflect time going? On your calendar, block off 20 minutes 1 month from now to review your notes in your journal (and these 3 weeks of the book if notes aren't enough of a reminder).

What do you predict will be your biggest impediment to maintaining and building momentum?

What steps can you take to sidestep that impediment?

WEEK 4
TEND TO YOUR EMOTIONS

Monday: Why it matters

It can be a little challenging to separate mind from emotions, they often are quite entangled. Your emotions, like your mind, are deeply influenced by your physical health. That's why we spent 2 of the 4 weeks of this month on physical health.

So, the first thing you can do to tend to your emotions is take care of your physical health.

If you've got a good rhythm going on physical activity, see if this week you can incorporate a little bit more movement.

Maybe it's raising your arms above your head throughout the day. Maybe it's skipping. Maybe it's taking a 2-minute walk or stretching break every hour. How can you get your body moving a little bit more, to better support your circulation systems that nourish your brain?

The other essential fundamental to steady emotions is a good night's sleep. Do you look at a screen within an hour of bed time? TV, phone, laptop? Can you start to close down the night without the screen time? You might have a physical or emotional addiction to this habit, given the nature of how those lights affect our brains. Be gentle with yourself as you incorporate manageable chunks of change.

Write down your plan for adding in a little more movement to your day. Write down your plan for taking out the screen time from that hour or so before bedtime so that your sleep can be a little more restful.

Tuesday: Good Old Self-Reflection

As you go through your day today, keep observation of your thoughts. Any time you notice a repeating thought or type of thought showing up that is detrimental in some way, write in down in your journal.

Once you get to the end of the day, finish the rest of this page.

Self-Reflection Exercise

Take a moment to get centered in your body through breathing. What happened right before the unhelpful thought occurred?

Why was that thought part of your response? Is it something from your childhood or an important relationship or a learned family behavior?

What is a thought that 'counters' that thought? (i.e., 'that person is so stupid' could be countered with. 'I know they are smart in some area of life, even if I can't see it.' Or 'I wonder what that person really thinks of me' could be countered with 'I respect myself, even when it's uncomfortable to worry that someone else might not respect me')

Write down the thought and your unique counter.

Come up with a game plan for re-training your brain to first, always give the counter, then over time, not have the thought in the first place.

If re-training your brain in this way is new to you, the first step is lots and lots of patience. It's all about learning to catch the thought, observe and accept it, then offer the counter.

Another technique I see having a lot of success is to thank the thought with something like 'Thank you. Your job is done, I don't need anything more from you right now.'

Wednesday: Keeping a Weather Eye on Stress

As a small business owner, your stress levels affect everything. Exercise can help you unload quite a bit of stress. With both employees and customers looking to you as the leader, you need to take care of your stress so that it does not negatively impact either of those relationships. Neither your employees nor your customers should ever experience you dumping your stress (of course there are always exceptions, but let's set the bar high).

But, while exercising immensely influences your stress levels, just exercising on a regular basis is not enough to successfully manage your stress. You also have to learn to be mindful of your stress (why mental exercise and unwind is so important), and self-reflect on what is creating it and what can be done about it. The exercise we did yesterday can have a huge long-term impact on stress levels, if you can have the patience to do the fine-grain work of catching, observing, and releasing those thoughts. But, today the focus is on the big-picture of noticing and eradicating stress.

Write down some of your observations about what throws you over the edge with stress, and how you 'dump' stress onto others.

Have your efforts to change how you exercise and eat affected your stress levels?

What is one reason that you use to justify dumping your stress onto others?

Can you take yourself outside of your perspective and come up with a reason for why that is something you need to address in order to improve the health of that relationship?

Congrats, you've been practicing deep level self-reflection! These skills are essential to getting through the material in this book, and to accelerating your business.

Thursday: A Sense of Play and Enjoyment

As human beings, if we aren't having fun living life, we are eventually going to self-sabotage in a major way. The stress could build up into a serious illness. We could drive away or alienate our loved ones. We could make some major, easily avoidable mistake with the business. Not feeling the simple joy of life, not feeling our unique sense of playful on a regular basis is going to have a negative impact on our business and seriously impede our capacity for growth.

Everyone's sense of playfulness and enjoyment looks different.

Take a moment to center yourself in your body and let your mind drift toward childhood. You can do this for the next few days as part of your evening wind-down. Think about what playful felt like inside. When did you feel at your most playful? What were you doing?

Who in your life brings out your sense of playfulness in a positive way? Whose sense of playfulness do you draw out? Do you have kids or a pet? How can you incorporate more time with this person or pet on a regular basis?

How do you have a sense of playfulness with yourself? It's important to have that as a part of alone time as it is with other people.

How can you bring a sense of light-heartedness to your workspace?

Let your mind mull over these questions and jot down thoughts or ideas as they pop up. From there you can create a plan for your manageable chunks of change.

Friday: Tying the Month Together

Week 1, we introduced the concept of manageable chunks of change as well as techniques for making changes to your physical fitness routine.

We talked about the importance of cultivating a curious and flexible mind.

We talked about the importance of a healthy emotional life through reflection and staying on top of stress.

All in all, we introduced a lot of concepts and went over a lot of changes to begin to make in your life.

Honest assessment, how is it all going? Are you working out more? Eating better? Sleeping better? Having more fun and practicing not taking life so seriously? Catching yourself with your bad mental habits?

As human beings, it's easy to have high motivation in the beginning, but then peter out as things go along and life happens. But as a business owner, it is essential that you develop the capacity to exercise discipline and judicious judgment when it comes to taking care of yourself. If you can do it for your body, you can handle anything when it comes to your business.

Go ahead, pat yourself on the back for all the changes you've begun.

Take a moment to catch your breath. Flip back through the reading and your notes for the past month. Enjoy your weekend! We're starting a whole new subject next week, and I want you to be able to keep the momentum going on your physical habits as we shift gears on tips and techniques for accelerating your business.

MONTH TWO
FAILING TO PLAN IS PLANNING TO FAIL

Failing to plan is planning to fail. Sounds simple, right?

And yet, of the dozens of people I've worked with, more often than not, there has been a failure to plan properly.

In the first week of this month on accelerating your business with better planning practices, we start with your role as the business owner. You are the visionary. If you don't have the vision, or take regular consistent time to hone your vision, troubleshoot, or develop implementation plans, then you are getting in your own way as a business owner. If you don't understand it's your job to have the vision, then you are going to struggle with planning and managing your time.

We start to take a look at the systems that your vision runs on. Your system of systems is what keeps the engine of your business growing in capacity, reach, and efficiency of effort. The health of your body and mind is the main fuel source, then after that comes how you manage and plan your time, and how you manage and plan your goals. Weeks 2 and 3 cover your system of systems from the perspective of the fundamental principles and concepts of time management and goal-setting. So if you've been diligently practicing 'manageable chunks of change' with keeping your body healthy, you are ready for this next step in accelerating your business. If 'manageable chunks of change' is a skill you are still building reps and expertise on, here is an opportunity to practice from a different angle.

Week 4 moves back from strategy to big-picture assessment. In this week we talk about how you need to have a process and plan for asking yourself on a regular basis, "Is my business complete?"

Taking the time for the big picture, assessing the systems, understanding reverse-engineering goals, and assessing the business overall makes all of the other tips and insights of this book more successful. I know it seems easier to take off running, or skip ahead to particular questions you have about an aspect of running a business you feel less knowledgeable about, but a strong foundational understanding of how to create the big picture, translate the vision into action, then assess makes you more efficient at all the other decisions you'll be making and skills you'll be developing as you work your way through this book.

WEEK 1
YOU ARE THE VISIONARY

Monday: Why does this matter to me?

A few years ago I started to think that maybe Facebook ads were drying out as a channel for generating leads. I'd been using it for 5-6 years at that point, and over the last couple years I was getting fewer and fewer leads.

Now, I could've just kept doing what I was doing and dismissed my observation about FB ads and just accepted that I was going to be getting fewer leads from that avenue and adjusted my money flow to either spend more on ads, less on ads, more on keeping the leads/customers that I have, or just accepted making less money and tightened the belt.

All of those might've meant my business could continue to survive, but they wouldn't have led to any sort of acceleration or growth, because all of them would be a passive acceptance of the status quo without tapping truly into my role and abilities as the visionary of my company.

But, because I have the habit of learning from other visionaries in a wide range of fields, business and otherwise, I knew I could find a way to turn my observation of Facebook ads becoming less of a source of revenue into a visionary opportunity.

I remembered coming across the name of Russell Brunson in one of the podcasts I follow. I'd remembered thinking that click funnels sounded interesting and viable, but at the time I hadn't moved forward with that observation. Now that it was time to reach a decision regarding my Facebook ads, I decided to research Brunson's vision for click funnels a little more thoroughly, and see if they could help me turn my problem with FB ads into an opportunity to accelerate my business.

And, it worked.

Having a clear understanding of your role as visionary helps you manage your time and resources to best effect. It is all too easy to become distracted, to put your time into avenues that don't maximize the success of your business. You need to understand that you are the visionary. You create and maintain the vision.

One of the things I hope you take away from that story is that you don't have to invent and visualize from scratch. That's also part of why we began the first month with health & mental fitness. If you are feeding your mind new ideas, and if you are getting regular inspiration and insight from those whose example motivates you and fires you up, then you will be naturally and intuitively developing your visionary instincts.

Take a minute to flip back to the week on keeping your mind sharp. Then look over your daily schedule and see where and how you can fit being inspired and motivated by others' excellence and success into your schedule. Personally, I love listening to podcasts while I work out and commute to work.

Maybe for you its while you cook or wind-down in the evening. Maybe you learn from socializing and need to join or create a group to get inspiration and creativity flowing in your day to day and week to week.

The other takeaway from my experience is that a vision is only worthwhile if it is translatable into strategy that gets implemented.

But first, take a moment to jot down some notes and observations to the following questions.

What value do you offer?

Who is your target market?

What distinguishes you from the competition?

What are your goals?

Who are your resources?

Do your answers roll readily off the tip of your tongue?

If not, take time to think through what your answers are. If not, you also need to take the time to understand *why* you don't know these things.

What beliefs or attitudes or habits prevent you from feeling self- assured and poised for success in your role as the visionary of your company?

Tuesday: Visionaries see the long-term

My father was a watchmaker. We didn't have a lot of toys, and I wanted to help my dad, so as a young kid, I would try to learn his craft. My dad started me off with bigger clocks, with bigger mechanical pieces so it was easier for me to learn the parts and how to move them. When I was 10 years old, it was my job to pull the bigger clocks apart, clean them, then put them back together.

This also kept me occupied while he focused on the intricate pieces of smaller watches. Building and fixing watches requires a lot of focus and attention.

Parents are visionaries for their kids. They have the vision and process for helping kids share the household load of chores, they plan what activities kids try to explore their interests, they teach kids how to handle money. The role of parent as visionary changes as children grow into adults, and of course children are encouraged to explore their interests, but it is parents who have the vision of how the world works, and parents who share that vision with their kids.

My dad envisioned me as his right-hand man. He used the vision to manage my time so he could invest his time on the more complicated projects. He saw my interest in helping, he saw a future with me as his right-hand man, and began to train me in a way that benefitted everyone.

If you want to scale up, you have to let others take over. Train them to do what is the least valuable use of your time.

Your work is to create expansion, to bring people to the door, and add value. It is also your role to

- o   make connections,
- o   have the ideas for marketing and customer satisfaction,
- o   inspect what you expect with staff, and
- o   strategize how to implement the vision.

My dad knew his son was his best connection for his vision of keeping the business in the family. He had the idea to start training me on easier tasks as a kid, and he always looked over my work and helped me grow my skills.

I meet a lot of business owners who let themselves get lost in the weeds of the daily operations or in the skies of the big dreams. Visionaries know how to balance the details, the concrete goals, with the imagination and ambition.

Start a new calendar in your online calendar system, or find a couple of blank months. Color code it for how you spent your business time the past 2 months.

- •   Blue for brainstorming, strategizing, troubleshooting, and research

- Yellow for day-to-day operations (i.e., updating website or storefront, interacting with customers, etc)
- Green for developing and implementing marketing strategies
- Purple for networking
- Red for distracting busywork

Your overall goal is to move to a balance of colors where yellow is minimal and mostly inspecting what you expect, and most of your time is blue or green.

So as we develop the skills of visionary leadership, your calendar will start to have a better balance of when and how your time goes to the day-to-day maintenance and when your time goes to brainstorming, creating, then visualizing and overseeing implementation of your new ideas for how to bring more people to your business and make them happier for having traded their money for your value.

Wednesday: Visionaries translate their goals into implementable steps

It's all well and good to have a color-coded picture of your real use of time, and a vision of how that picture needs to change.

What really makes visionaries succeed is mastering the art and science of translating goals into action.

All of this book is geared toward training you on those skills, starting with manageable chunks of change and self-reflection.

Monday, we took a snapshot of your vision. Tuesday, we took a snapshot of your reality. Today, I want you to be free form in your reflection and observation (try to minimize the analysis). You can get as creative as you like. Maybe you draw a picture of Monday's observations and then look at the 2 pictures side-by-side. Maybe you create a color-coding system for Monday. Maybe you jot down thoughts that pop up as you go throughout the day. Maybe you find people to discuss with (again, minimizing analysis at this point).

These are the first 2 steps of translating the vision into action: developing the picture of where you want to go, and the picture of where things are at now. When you can step back and reflect on those two pictures, you allow your creative brain to bring forth solutions. That's the hardest skill to master, because it requires a lot of patience and honesty.

Thursday: Visionaries know how to handle their own discomfort

A few years ago I listened to Damon Jon speak. He was on stage telling his story of how he went from nothing to a multi-millionaire. Listening to the details of his story, the passion and intensity, the struggles and the victories inspired me to get out of my comfort zone and strive for more. Just like we talked about yesterday, you need to keep feeding your fire of determination.

There is another aspect to knowing how to handle your own discomfort that we began to address Monday: being willing to embrace the discomfort of challenges that land on our doorstep.

About 9 years ago my business was singing everything was so smooth. I was making enough money to be able to do all these cool things like traveling, etc.

And then a competitor opened up right across the street from me.

I thought, 'Oh my god, I gotta get my shit together, because now I'm going to be splitting my profits.' I got out of my comfort zone, started hustling, putting my time into my business. My numbers weren't growing, it was the same as when I was comfortable.

And then another place opened up same concept a few blocks away. Talk about uncomfortable!

I knew it was time to really focus on lead generation and marketing.

Then, a year later another store opened up nearby. A place opened up specifically on one of my products. Niche-specific. I about busted my jaw it dropped so fast and hard to the floor when I heard. 3 stores to compete with...I was living with discomfort every day.

I realized to my core how important it is for small business owners to be dynamic rather than static. When you're dynamic, you are ready to embrace the challenge. During those years I had to figure out how to go from being comfortably successful to being ready to learn, change, adapt. If I was static, doing the same thing over and over again, ignoring the fact that change was needed, worst case my business would have closed; best case I'd feel the constant pinch of money uncertainty.

When change is needed you have to be dynamic and start making changes. I started implementing strategies that will drive traffic to my business. I started doing research on my competitors to see how they are doing things, to see what I'm doing that they're not doing.

Keep dynamic and keep testing to find how to translate the uncomfortable into opportunity. Testing isn't always comfortable. Learning new things isn't always comfortable.

I was lucky that when this happened, I'd already learned from Damon Jon to get out of my comfort zone and push limits. I wanted to surpass what he has, not from greed, but from the desire to strive for what's better. That desire for excellence was what helped me be dynamic and willing to be uncomfortable and making changes to my business to not only keep up, but thrive, with the times.

Think about what's happened with your business over the last year. When and what major obstacles have shown up? Did you run from your discomfort or were you dynamic and willing to test new things? Be honest! If you're not honest about where you are at, it's a lot harder to change.

When you felt that discomfort, what went through your mind? What are some ways you can remind yourself to be dynamic?

Be creative.

What is the most uncomfortable aspect of lead generation for you?

Friday: Self-Reflect and Strategize

Looking back over the past 2 work weeks, list every task you have spent time on in your business as well as how much time you spent.

Now, categorize each task into 'creating expansion,' 'bringing people to the door,' 'adding value to our products/services,' 'networking,' 'strategizing,' 'training staff,' 'getting eyeballs on,' 'resting and recharging,' 'administrative maintenance.'

Which tasks could you delegate right now? Which tasks can you set a goal for delegating in 6 months? Which tasks do you avoid because their uncomfortable? Which tasks do you obsess over getting done perfectly?

We'll use your answers to implement a time management strategy later this month. Let your answers simmer. Jot down more stuff as it occurs to you.

WEEK 2
VISIONARIES USE AND CREATE SYSTEMS

Monday: Why does this matter to me?

Having a written documentation of your systems for every domain of your business saves you time and money in all kinds of ways. When you don't know your systems, you don't know what is or isn't working, you don't have a starting place for evaluating. Systems help you keep track of your time, your money, your successes and your failures.

You need systems for lead generation. You need systems for staff hiring, training, and expectations. You need systems for client retention. You need systems for bookkeeping, for keeping track of client data, expenses, income streams, and for how technology is used in your business.

Your systems should help you save your time and effort that then becomes invested into your tasks as a visionary. Having your systems written down makes it easier to hand off tasks to staff and be a good boss.

Part of keeping track of your systems means creating categories for the types of work that need to be done.

Your systems should also keep track of time. Everything on your list and breakdown of your systems should include how much time needed, who is responsible, and what the deadlines are.

You also need a system for research and your personal time and health. Having a business that is scalable and expanding requires regular learning of new skills, and it means that you are happy and healthy.

Tuesday: Time Management Systems

Tackling how you plan your time is your first system to hone. Once you automate these systems they will turn your time around from putting out fires to being fast and flexible when those inevitable surprises (both good and bad) show up.

Pull out your calendar. Block off 30 minutes Monday morning or Sunday evening for 30 minutes of looking ahead to the week.

Create a short agenda for yourself for this meeting. Make it problem-solving oriented. Use the categories from last week to help you design your agenda. Make sure your plan for the week connects to your quarterly plan and your yearly plan (if you don't yet have these plans, we get to them next week). Once you get used to taking the time for this weekly focus meeting, you might not always need 30 minutes.

Every weekly focus meeting agenda should start with reviewing the quarterly goals and what is your priority for the week for achieving those goals. Every agenda should also include an honest assessment of what happened, successful or a failure, from the week before.

Visionaries look ahead to the future as well as back to the past, to make the most of the moment.

Wednesday: Maximize Time, Minimize 'Noise'

I am a big believer in using a calendar software program. I use Google Calendar. It links with a ton of different software systems (that we start to discuss and implement in the months ahead). Having a software program for your calendar saves you a ton of time in the long run. Even if you still plan to use a paper calendar, you are going to want to start using an online calendar especially if you or your staff work with clients, and especially if you want your business to be scalable.

You are going to want to automate that calendar as much as possible. If you have meetings with staff, have them at the same time every week and make it so that only the most serious of reasons lead to a reschedule. You can also use your calendar to have regular time blocked off for the different facets of running your business. Doing a similar sort of task at the same time every day, week after week, helps train your brain for maximum efficiency—just like getting out of bed and working out does for your physical health.

You can use some of the categories I've suggested, or you can create your own category system. All I want is for you to no longer waste time, be that on emails, internet black holes of social media or article overdosing, or however else your time gets sucked up by minutiae.

Yesterday I asked you to get started automating a weekly focus meeting with yourself. Tomorrow, I'm going to set up a better way for starting and ending your work days. Today, I want you to look at your weekly calendar and determine how you can make it as regular and automated as possible.

If you see clients, set regular hours of availability. If you are always making exceptions, troubleshoot why you do that.

If you have a lot of email correspondence, social media presence, website updating, set regular hours.

Set regular blocks for being creative, brainstorming, etc. Set regular blocks for bookkeeping.

Set regular hours for research and regular hours for developing and implementing marketing campaigns.

It's going to take some trial and error. It's going to take some exploring your own discomfort. It's going to take learning new skills.

But, I promise you, if you start to automate your time in blocks, you will see massive increases in efficiency.

Add 'troubleshooting my time-blocking' to your weekly focus meeting for the next month's worth of agendas, to reinforce and maximize your development of calendar mastery.

Thursday: Start and end your work day for maximum efficiency

In addition to a weekly planning meeting, you should start and end your day with a quick meeting with yourself. If you need to, put it on your calendar so you get a reminder.

Without a system for assessment of how your day went, and one for prioritizing what needs to be accomplished that day, your time is at the whim of events. Visionaries protect and direct their own time.

Do you currently start the day by opening your email? If so, you aren't protecting your time, you are letting others direct your time. Put a sticky note where ever it is that you start your day. Write something like, "What are my 3 priorities for today?" Begin to start your day with answering the question. Doing it in writing, whether on paper, in a planner, or electronically gives you data to review in your weekly meetings, and will help you figure out what you can delegate, and what eats up, or disrupts your plan.

At the end of the day, jot down a few sentences of assessment of how the day went. Create and implement your plan for maintaining and sustaining this new habit over the long haul.

Friday: Maintain and sustain your new skills as a planner of your time

You have your first meeting with yourself after the weekend is over. Have you gathered all the materials you need? Have you made it as easy as possible for yourself to have a good meeting? Put the book down for

5 minutes and gather everything you need for the meeting. If you are likely to forget, set a reminder for yourself.

Did you do a quick assessment at the end of the day yesterday? Have you set your 3 priorities for today? Do that now, too.

If you didn't do what I just asked you to do, or you haven't begun a daily 5-10 minutes of planning priorities and assessing the day, take a few minutes to reflect on why not in your journal. If you did do it, reflect on how it felt. Did you feel like you had more control over your time, and therefore your vision?

Now write about how having a daily and weekly plan will help you maintain the vision.

Pull open the Small Profit Arsenal FB group (you should have a link directly into the group in your bookmarks toolbar so you don't get distracted by your FB feed. Don't check your notices or your messages, go directly to the group and exit out of FB when your done. Protect your time). Share a little bit of your reflection, ask questions, maybe take a couple minutes to read what others have written and comment. Or, connect with some sort of accountability partner.

Lastly, reflect on what is going to be the hardest part of staying consistent with this new method of planning and organizing your time with daily and weekly check-ins. Are you likely to forget? Do you feel this isn't a good use of your time? What can you do to build it into an automatic step? How can you plan ahead to make this work best for you and your vision for your business?

WEEK 3
REVERSE ENGINEER YOUR GOALS

Monday: Why does this matter to me?

Your goals are born from your vision. Your systems are what you do repeatedly to achieve your current goals. As the visionary, you must always be looking ahead into the unknown, translating your vision into goals, and goals into strategies.

The best way to do that is to reverse engineer your goals. Where do you want to be in a year? What needs to be in place in the last quarter of the year? For that to be in place in the last quarter, what needs to happen this quarter? What do you need to be learning or creating a system for next week in order to make that happen?

Finalized and polished goals are measurable specifics at the yearly and quarterly level. Time needs to be set aside every quarter and year for an honest assessment—which means seeing mistakes objectively, as information to help troubleshoot and learn for the next quarter. (Pull your calendar out and block out the time now for quarterly and yearly assessments)

Without reverse engineering, you won't have a clear sense of how much time, energy, learning, money, etc., your vision needs. Without reverse engineering, you don't have a clear process for assessing the feasibility of your goals.

I don't have much 'work' for you to do today, tomorrow, and Wednesday for two reasons. 1, so you can keep building momentum with everything from the past couple weeks by taking a bit of a breather, and 2, because you don't want to get ahead of yourself on reverse engineering your goals. Taking the time to think things through carefully and really let those creative juices marinate leads to bigger success than hurrying.

Tuesday: Categorize Your Goals

All your goals should revolve around a central vision of what you want your business to look like in 1-3 years in terms of income, customers and effect on the world. Then, those goals get separated into separate sections. There should be goals for staff training and skills to develop or maintain. There should be goals for lead generation and client retention. There should be goals to increase the value of what you offer. There should be goals related to new skills to master.

Take what you wrote for the vision for your company and break it down into goals for staff, lead generation/retention, and increasing the value of your offering.

Next, break each goal down into a list of skills to master, current strengths to leverage, lessons learned from past mistakes, resources, and how much time each project will take.

Based on your vision, which is the biggest priority? Which will require most of your time? How much can you hand off to staff to implement?

Set this information aside to incorporate into your weekly check-in, and decide what you need to prioritize with the rest of this week to begin to reverse-engineer your priority goals.

Wednesday: Example of Reverse Engineering a Goal

Let's say you want to start making $1000 more dollars a month within the next year.

In order to do that, you have a number of different options.

You can create an incentive for customer referral with your current loyal group of regulars.

You can upsell current customers on additional products or services.

You can offer a new product.

You can create a promotion or special, or update current promotions to bring new leads into the door.

You can also do a combination of those to hit your target.

It is helpful to think about what has been most successful in the past. As you get better at tracking which leads to more business, you will be more efficient at scaling your business. All of the options need to be part of the overall plan, but for right now, let's focus on building just one of these.

Let's say you have a ton of customers who buy single passes at a time for your services, on a random basis. You also offer a membership to your business, and you have several events a year that you could increase attendance on. You've decided the best way to hit your year target of $1,000 more in income is to upsell to your current customers, rather than work to get more people in the door. You want to start with increasing the sense of investment and satisfaction of your current customer base.

First, you'd brainstorm everything you could do to encourage them to become more invested in your business. Brainstorming might include researching or asking other people who've succeeded for this for some advice and strategies.

As you brainstorm, you realize your staff have no trained skills to encourage clients to purchase the membership option. So, you might decide that for this next quarter, you need to develop and implement a new training program for your staff. The second quarter, you would implement and troubleshoot, and at the end of the quarter get feedback from both customers and staff on the success, including looking at the conversion rates of your staff (remember, you need concrete measurable things to determine what is and isn't working). If one staff member has a high conversion rate, find out what they are doing differently and see if you can have them train your other staff members. Or, free up their time from other duties and give them more time to upsell.

If you don't have any employees to delegate to, you are going to have to take a look at your entire set of yearly goals and determine how much time you have to add to upselling. Maybe you need to invest time into getting trained on upselling by someone who is successful at it. Research various people and determine what your potential return on investment of your time and money are going to be and whether or not that is going to help you meet your goal of 1,000 more dollars income every quarter within the next year.

Thursday: Implement

Put the information you've gathered this week into your agenda for your next weekly focus meeting. Begin thinking and jotting down notes for how to make the most use of your time now. Write down everything that needs to be accomplished, then the order things need to be accomplished in. Make sure to plan time for research if you realize you need to research.

Creating a yearly goal, then breaking it down into quarterly tasks, then breaking those tasks down into new skills needed, time for research, time for letting the creativity out, plus keeping on top of everything else takes practice. Don't worry about getting it perfect the first time, just start to build the skill and learn as you go.

Friday: Reflect and Strategize

Learning to reverse engineer your goals takes trial and error. There are a lot of moving parts, and often a lot of new skills to learn or to train your staff on. Look back through the material and what you've written.

What skills do you already have as a visionary? What skills do you not have? What about your mindset needs to shift?

We often use time as an excuse and a scapegoat, rather than an ally and an asset. In learning about being a visionary, developing and refining your systems, and reverse-engineering your goals, what beliefs or attitudes about time have come up?

Time to shift your mindset. Create a mantra that reflects your new attitude toward time into your weekly meeting. Switching to an expansive, can-do mindset about time will help you better lean in to your new role as visionary as well as think more clearly about your goals, systems, and planning their expansion.

Some sample mantras include:

- I get everything accomplished that I need to in a timely manner.
- I view time as an ally and resource.
- I am a master of determining how to use time to best effect.

You want your statements to have simple, present-tense verbs and be positive and action-oriented, not negative. Add reading or stating this sentence aloud to your agenda for next week.

Repetition is an essential ally when it comes to shifting your mindset.

WEEK 4
IS YOUR BUSINESS COMPLETE?

Monday: Stay Organized

Do you have a clear and easy-to-understand checklist of everything your business needs for success? Is that checklist written down, easily accessible? How does the checklist show up in your planning, goal-setting, and working with staff?

Look over this starter checklist. Plan a meeting with yourself or your team to discuss how your business measures up to this checklist.

- Searchable online
- Solid calendar
- Work space
- Presence on relevant social media platforms
- Restrooms Working website (mobile-friendly)
- Reception area
- Lead generation strategies
- CRM software
- Accounting system
- Documentation of business systems

Start brainstorming your checklist in your journal. Once you've got it finalized (taking your time, prioritizing getting it right over getting it fast), where does it need to live? Plan a meeting with yourself or your team to discuss how your business measures up to this checklist.

You can flip through the rest of the book for ideas on what else your business needs to be complete.

Having this kind of list and looking at it, updating it by seeing what needs to be added, removed, or modified is a great way to set the stage in your quarterly or yearly planning sessions.

Tuesday: Documenting how things work

A couple weeks ago we talked about how it is important to have written down how everything works and what the processes are. This allows new employees an easy starting point, and gives you a clear reference point for deciding what changes need to be made.

A lot of people resist doing this because it feels time-consuming. But investing the time on the front end saves you time in the long-run (a skill we will come back to time and again). **Documentation forces you to confront all the hidden weaknesses of how your business operates.**

Create a plan and block off time for creating a document with all of your processes. If you can, delegate it.

Microsoft Word or Google Docs are great programs for this, because then it can be a living document, with notes and links.

If you don't have time for this, you can block off the time for it later. You are the master of your calendar and your time. I'm just teaching you how to automate.

Wednesday: Practice Using Your List to Evaluate and Plan What Needs Doing

One facet of this list is maintaining the professional face and accessibility of your business. Ask your staff or some of your customers their opinions about the elements on the checklist. Can you take the time this quarter to update any of those that need updating? Can you delegate this task? If all or most of these need updating, which is your biggest priority based on your goals for the next year? Is this something that can wait until next quarter?

Write your customer/staff feedback in your journal, as well as your own assessments.

Do you need to do some more extensive market research on one or more of these for more information on how to make the best updates to the items on this list? If so, plot out your plan, estimate how much time needed. Note who you can delegate this to.

Do a cost analysis of making your desired change based on the assessments.

Thursday: Breath, Orient, Assess

We are learning how to incorporate new ideas and options for making changes into the big picture, which requires retraining your brain and sticking to your weekly and daily goals as well as reverse-engineering so you know how much time, energy, and care you can and should invest in any one thing, based on the reality of your business and your current available resources.

Add consideration of your desired change to your next weekly focus meeting's agenda.

Maybe for you that agenda is determining research priorities. Maybe it's blocking off time for self-reflection and assessment. Maybe it is using the checklist against your 1-year goals to determine a new quarterly strategy.

Your checklist is your living representation of your business. It's a map, a picture. Having a reflection of your business in this format creates opportunity for your creative and analytical brains to work together to determine how to manage and wield your time.

Friday: Reflect and Digest The Month

Today, we are looking back over the whole month, to see how our brains have begun to work differently. Regular self-assessment makes those changes stick deeper into our consciousnesses.

Becoming a Visionary

What have you noticed about taking on this new role as visionary? What new skills have you developed? Do you carry yourself differently around customers or staff? What new thoughts have you noticed? Has it changed how you use your time and set your goals?

Building your Visionary Use of Time

Write down how many times you stuck to your weekly plan. Write down how many times you stuck to your morning prioritizing and end-of-day reflection.

Did you hit at least 75%? If so, you are well on track with incorporating these methods for accelerating your business. Have a great weekend and an excellent weekly focus meeting.

If you haven't, you have the opportunity here to learn how to incorporate failure into the long-term success, something every entrepreneur must know. Time to troubleshoot.

What got in the way?

What's the excuse you are making to yourself? What beliefs or attitudes are holding you back?

Is it that you haven't fully understood some of the concepts? Block out time to do research or get onto the Small Profit Business Arsenal page to troubleshoot your process with the group.

Reverse Engineering Your Goals

What is your 1-year goal for expanding your business?

How does that break down into measurable quarterly strategies?

What steps do you need to take next week to stay on track?

Look over your plan of implementing your reverse-engineered goal. Can you break it down into smaller tasks? Can you find anything else to delegate? Can you refine your estimates on how your time will be used? Do you have a process in place, or a time blocked out later on for assessing the success of your new plan to achieve your goal?

MONTH THREE
CARING FOR YOUR STAFF

Your central task as the leader of your business is to be the visionary, and hand off work—through proper training—to the largest extent possible. Switching more of your time to being creative and developing the goals and plans to implement that creativity to increase sales means you need to have a staff with a sense of excellence to handle the day-to-day tasks. When your staff are thoroughly trained and competent in their roles, not only does it free up your time, but a strong staff builds the reputation of your business and increases your value.

Even if you don't currently have staff, there are still people you work with, and you can still train them to better meet the needs of your business. Everyone you work with to help your business be more successful can benefit from you improving in your role as a leader of leaders—as the person who builds trust, demands consistency and a strong work ethic, and provides clarity for how things should be run.

Where ever you are in staffing your business, you need to think of the process in terms of systems and of evaluating the system. Every aspect of your business needs a plan, and needs to be part of your visionary process of generating the vision and translating the vision into strategy.

WEEK 1
MANIFEST YOUR CORE VALUES

Monday: Why does this matter to me?

When I was training at the martial arts studio, I started teaching after I got my red belt, at 14 years old. I started teaching the youngest kids. At that time, we didn't use lesson plans or do much prior preparation for class—for me as a student, with homework and family responsibilities, it wasn't like I had much time for that anyways.

One of the benefits of learning to teach by just winging it, was that I learned a lot about really listening to the students. In order to know what to teach, I had to observe what they could do. And we knew how to have fun! It's so much easier to relax and connect when the back of your mind isn't churning up about whether or not you're meeting your predetermined goals.

I winged it through the first years of running my first business.

Winging it works great in terms of getting things moving forward, and at the beginning of your business, it is easy to think that it's enough, that your own drive to succeed and willingness to sit down and do the work will be enough.

And it's important to be able to handle things on the fly as they show up. It's so, so crucial. But it doesn't accelerate your business.

Let's get oriented to how your staff is working right now.

Write down the name of everyone who does work for you, and list their main responsibility. You should be able to list everything in one concise sentence. Everyone's name should come readily to mind. If you have to think about it, and revise the sentence, that's okay for now, but it is a sign that you are winging it when it comes to staff, and getting in your own way of accelerating your business

Now next to each name, list 2 strengths and 2 weaknesses. Underline the names of everyone who is a natural leader (i.e., they have initiative, they suggest ideas for improving the business, they bring in or retain clients or customers based on their unique way of relating to people).

6 months from now, everyone on that list can be underlined.

All it takes is sticking to your role as visionary.

As you work with more people and you have staff turnover, and as you get to further know your staff, and they start to blossom, this list will change. Take some time right now to incorporate this type of staff assessment into your timeline. Maybe this is a yearly or bi-yearly task. Maybe it is pulled out every time you have a new hire. Having a written document is fuel for your creative brain. It will help you with training, with determining how to implement marketing strategies, with determining your quarterly strategies. Right now, though, I just want you to focus on automating when and how the list gets updated.

Tuesday: Core Values and Communication

How many people that work for you know exactly what you think of their strengths and weaknesses?

Write down why or why not. What is it about your leadership skills that leads you to be this kind of communicator with your staff?

Write down your current system for giving feedback on strengths and weaknesses to your staff. Do you email? Give off- the-cuff feedback? Do you have a weekly or monthly system?

Give feedback both spontaneously and systematically. All of your staff should know that you know the strengths and weaknesses of every team member. When your staff knows that you see what they bring to the table, they will naturally have more motivation and work to imitate your leadership style.

If you don't give spontaneous feedback to staff in front of other staff/clients, then take a moment to think about how you might begin to do that. What skills do you need to develop to make that happen?

If you don't give systematic feedback privately to staff, add prepping this task to your next weekly focus meeting. We'll talk more about it during the rest of this week.

Wednesday: Leadership

I started at the martial arts studio when I was 12. I started teaching at 14, and became official staff when I was 15. I was waiting tables to make enough money for classes, but I wanted to become more involved, and take the time I was spending waiting tables and investing it further into the studio and my martial arts skills.

When Master Chhe took over the studio, he started to bring more of a focus to the business aspect of a studio: marketing and client retention and making sure to watch the money flow. We started having weekly meetings shortly after I became part of the staff, and I learned a lot about running a business from the inside, without formal training. I had a natural drive to work hard, and have always been a self-starter, and had an amazing opportunity at a young age.

You want to hire people with these talents, but you can also foster and instill them in anybody. Every human being has the capacity to be a leader. If you have a vision, and you work on your communication skills and setting a consistent example with a clear plan, then your staff will develop their unique leadership abilities.

Let's start with your employee with the least demonstrated ability to lead.

It's time to get really honest with yourself. Do you treat them as if you expect them to be a leader, or do you fall into the trap of believing their story about their timidity, foolishness, or inability to learn to take initiative?

What is one key task that they consistently fail to meet your expectations on? Write it in as clear and short and kind a sentence as you can.

Pick a time this week when you will be able to talk to them alone for a few minutes.

Ask them what they like most about the job. Ask them what their favorite thing to learn about the business is.

Tell them you'd like to give them the opportunity to learn more of that, but that they are going to have to improve their abilities in other areas. Make sure they understand that they are going to have to work to earn the reward.

Tell them you want to have a sit-down meeting next week to discuss the planned changes. Put them in charge of the meeting. Say something like, "I want you to feel like this business matters as much to you as to me. I know that will happen when you get to learn and be creative in the area of your choosing. But part of any job is learning how to get better at the work we don't like to do. When we have our meeting next week, I want you to come prepared to explain to me what your plan is for getting better at_____part of this job. I will make sure you have opportunity to master the skills you need.

Come with questions for me, and a self-assessment of why you think you aren't as good at this part of the business, as well as the start of a plan for how to change things. Once I see that you are serious about this, we will start to give you more responsibilities and fun in the area that you care about."

After you have this chat, pull out your journal and reflect about how the meeting went. How do you think your leadership skills were? Could you improve your communication?

What did you notice about how they responded to you? Did they seem like they became more invested in doing a good job? Whatever your answer to the question is, you need to be prepared to address it clearly and with compassion.

Schedule a time to prep for the meeting. Get feedback from a mentor or a trusted employee.

Make sure you have a plan for understanding and supporting their learning style. You might consider having them take one of the many personality tests out there, such as Gallup, or the Dynamic Wealth Test. You might consider having all of your staff doing so, and building it into your meeting or training system. Having a common language of strengths and styles improves how your team works together.

Thursday: Develop Your Staff

Now that we've practiced designing and implementing a plan for one employee, it is time to do the same for the rest.

How often do you need to meet with each employee individually?

How often do you need to meet with everyone as a team?

Create a structure for a meeting agenda for individual and group meetings. It should include reflecting on what's happened since the past meeting, discussing the plan for upcoming projects, and encouraging them to ask honest questions and give open feedback on how they feel they are developing as employees.

Ask your employees to develop a 6-month goal of skills that they would like to develop. Include discussion of their skill-building as part of the meetings.

Even if you don't have staff, you can adapt these lessons to anyone you work with as part of your business.

Friday: Strategize

What needs to be on the agenda of your next weekly meeting in terms of prepping for these changes in how you work with staff and others?

How much time do you need to set aside for creating your vision for your staff to develop as leaders?

What is your 6-month goal for your employees? How do you need to include this reverse-engineering into your long-term and short-term plans?

What strengths and skills do you need to develop in order to better support your staff's growth as leaders? Create a plan for developing this. What resources can you leverage? Be sure to include channels for receiving honest feedback on your development.

WEEK 2
CORE VALUES & BUILDING TRUST

Monday: Why This Matters

Without open lines of communication between you and your staff, nobody is going to be able to develop as effective leaders, and your vision for your company is going to stall out.

One of the main tasks as the visionary leader of your staff is setting the example in terms of instilling and fostering the trust that is so crucial to a value-adding work environment.

I set the example with the 11 core values of my brand. I send a weekly email to my staff that briefs them on upcoming promotions, tasks, reminders, praise, etc. Every email, every week, I start that email with mentioning one of those core values.

Having core values is like the 10 commandments of the workplace. They keep the boundaries on expectations clear, simple, and straightforward. They make an easy reference point for praise, criticism, and training. They are an essential part of the interview process because they let potential workers know what to expect. Clearly stated core values that are nonnegotiable are the foundation of trust and clear communication between you and your staff.

Here are the first 5 of my core values:

o   Treat everyone with respect. Be humble, have humility.
o   Accept responsibility. If you've done something incorrectly, don't play the blame game; be responsible.

o Take initiative. If you see something needs to be done, take care of it instead of looking for others or ignoring it.
o Be reliable and accountable. When you've committed to do something, follow through. Protect the integrity of your promises.
o Be coachable. Constructive criticism is welcomed when you are eager to learn and accept the responsibility of a job.

They are simple, direct, and easy to remember. It will take some development for you to finalize your core values, and then to integrate in a simple, easeful way, but once you've incorporated your core values, your communication with your staff will become so much more efficient. Efficiency, economy of effort streamlines your business. The simpler you can make staff communication, the more you can focus on getting people in the door and on having them walk out happy they came in.

You don't want to rush the creation of your core values. There is no set or 'right' number of core values. Often, the best starting place is to ask your employees or close friends and family what they see as the core values of your business. Start with the strengths. Then think about the things you have to remind staff about over and over, what value of your business isn't getting clearly expressed?

Use your journal to make some notes. Pull out your planner and put it on your weekly focus meeting agenda to sift through the notes, data, and generative brainstorming you do. Maybe you need to schedule in time to ask questions of employees and others. Maybe you need to schedule in some brainstorming time into your week. Keep your notebook handy so that you can pull it open and jot down thoughts as they come to you throughout the day.

Remember, your core values are part of your unique vision. The words should resonate with who you are as a person.

Tuesday: Improve Trust By Being Willing to Change

Take a moment to reflect on how you react when someone tells you something you don't want to hear—both bad news and criticism. Do some breathing and calming exercises. Let your mind empty out a bit before beginning the reflection. The more tranquil you can be, the more open to self-honesty and new thoughts you will be.

Come up with a new small strategy for responding to improve your ability to react with patience and calm to bad news. The more skillful you are at this, the more open your employees will be to receiving constructive criticism, and they will also be more motivated to work hard for your company.

Your strategy might be to count to 10. It might be changing what the first words out of your mouth are to something like, "Thank you for bringing this to my attention." It might be verbalizing one of your core values. Whatever it is, test it out, practice it. Give it a solid effort, if it isn't working, try another or find someone to troubleshoot with.

Wednesday: Inspect What You Expect

A friend of mine used to work at a coffee shop that used a spiral notebook for staff to communicate with each other. The notebook was full of the cranky, experienced employees shouting or passive-aggressively shaming the newbies. They got rid of the notebook after the manager left. Things didn't really improve, though.

They switched to having 2 meetings. One after the transition to the lighter summer season when everyone was out of town, the second after the transition to the busy fall season when kids were back in school and it started to get cold. Now, these meetings were in no way an improvement over the notebook of shaming. Can you guess why?

Because the meetings happened *after* the seasonal change. The bosses held the meetings after everyone had been messing up, and just ended up yelling at them in between the oreo cookie of a fun food-filled opener and the socializing, relaxing game time closer to the meeting.

The nice, sweet outsides of the meetings didn't really show respect or accountability. The bosses made employees feel bad for not knowing what they thought they should know without making their expectations clear and inspecting what they expect.

If they'd had the meetings *before* the seasonal transition, they could have prepared staff for what was ahead, trained, outlined expectations. Then, they could have inspected what they expected as the shift happened, rather than letting it build up into serious messes and then essentially yelling at staff only to repeat it all over again in 6 months. You probably wouldn't be surprised to learn that employees who'd been there awhile started finding reasons for not going to those meetings.

When you have clear core values that you regularly emphasize with your staff, you have a foundation for outlining what you expect from their work. Once they know what to expect, you inspect it at regular intervals.

Inspecting what you expect is not just for meetings. It's all the time. It's your business. Nobody cares more about your business than you do. So when you care enough to always be inspecting for excellence, your staff is going to pick up the habit.

For example, say you have a core value of 'the store always looks professional and inviting' and you've been busy launching a new campaign so you didn't notice that the front counter had started to become dirty and disorganized. The mess probably started small, a customer spilt a little coffee, or left a stack of fliers in disarray. Next thing you know, it's spread across 10 feet of counter. You weren't inspecting what you expect, and you weren't balancing your priority of launching a campaign with inspecting what you expect. So you have to get really good at going back to the drawing board and coming up with more and more efficient ways of communicating your values and expectations and inspecting them.

In that scenario, if the coffee shop had core values that the boss regularly emphasized, and had meetings laying out what the boss expected at the change in business with the seasons, then the boss regularly inspected the store for his expectations, everyone would have been a lot happier.

Thursday: Explain Why It's Important

In addition to having values that you emphasize on a regular basis, laying out your expectations, and inspecting what you expect, you will have a better time of it if you explain why it's important.

When employees know what the impact of their efforts is on the long-term success of the business, then they are naturally going to be more motivated and inspired to excellence.

Think back over the last 2 months. How often did you explain why a certain task, or improvement to how they do things is important to the business? When you did so, based on your observation of them as a person as well as the changes in their behavior, how would you rate the effectiveness of your communication?

Look over your plans for interacting with employees in the next 2 weeks. When and how can you test new ways of expressing the importance of their efforts? How will you know you've done a good job?

Come up with a brief plan for implementing this new information successfully into your interactions with employees. Look at your calendar and block out time for the different components of building this plan: creative genesis, goal-setting, trouble-shooting, implementing, researching, etc.

Friday: Constructive Criticism

You must develop 3 skills: providing constructive criticism, making sure staff know it is okay to fail sometimes, and encouraging everyone to have a learner mindset.

Describe your current method of providing constructive criticism. What system do you use?

How do you give orders or tell your staff when they are doing something incorrectly? Do you get impatient and snap? What causes you to lose your temper or be short with your staff?

Are you always in a hurry? Do you take time to chat with your employees and ask them sincere questions about their personal lives? Do you say please and thank you with sincerity? Do you look your staff in the eyes when you give compliments?

Take a few minutes to reflect on your patterns of behavior with your staff. Identify 2-3 small changes you can begin to implement today. Make a note for the agenda of your next weekly meeting to reflect on how the changes went. Create reminders for yourself so you don't slip back into old habits.

Write down 1 goal for improving how you communicate constructive criticism.

How do you think your staff perceives your response to failure? Your staff will trust you more if they perceive that you see failure as a learning opportunity. Have any mistakes been made by staff in the last week or so? Is there a big or new project coming up where you can anticipate some mistakes being made? Create a strategy for teaching your staff to see the mistake as an opportunity for learning.

Create a mantra for yourself to use to quickly take charge of the situation and put your staff at ease when a mistake has been made (i.e., FAIL = First Mistakes In Learning; 'every scar is a lesson learned. What lesson did you learn from this?')

WEEK 3
MEETINGS, DELEGATION, STRATEGY

Monday: Why This Matters

A good structure for meetings, task delegation, and strategizing goes a long way in terms of work efficiency. Refining and automating these systems frees up precious time and mental energy for other tasks you are responsible for.

As you train and encourage your staff to be leaders, you want to consider handing them more responsibility for meetings and providing input on the short- and long-term strategies for your business. The perspectives and insights of your employees are a precious resource.

I have a weekly meeting plus a weekly email briefing. Even when I was at my business all day every day in the beginning, I still held a weekly meeting. They help build cohesion, trust, and inspiration, catch issues before they start to become major problems, and a lot of creative ideas get generated at meetings.

Tuesday: Structure and Timing of Meetings

Meetings follow a simple structure. We socialize and share at the beginning. Encourage everyone to talk at least a little during this time with round-robin type-activities, or you can have it be more free form. It depends on you and your people. I have a large staff, so we do quick round-robin shares of what's been new and exciting in our personal lives.

Second, I give announcements, updates. Then we look at whatever is on the calendar for the next few weeks (or months if it is a big promotion like a New Year's sale). I hand out tasks, we troubleshoot, they ask questions, brainstorm. Then we do a training or skill-building activity. I like to ask employees when we are in 1-1 conversations if they have anything they'd like to learn, get better at, or lead a training on for others. We close with shout outs for something particularly well done.

On a semi-regular basis for my training/skill-building activity I will play a game where they get to practice constructive criticism. Everyone shares a compliment and a request for improvement. Compliments or requests can be specific to one person or to the room or a group. If I feel that people are avoiding naming someone, I will ask, "Is there anyone in the room that you'd like to address directly?" I'll follow the question up with a reference to a core value, "We are all coachable here. It's a sign of respect to directly address your points."

Practicing positive and negative feedback as a group drains the tension and naturally encourages them to speak directly to their coworkers in more informal settings.

Take a look at how you organize and schedule meetings. Pick 1-2 things to make improvements on.

If you keep a consistent structure for meetings, they will be more efficient in the long run, because staff will know what to expect and naturally be more prepared for them than if they are randomly scheduled and haphazardly conducted.

Wednesday: Gather Employee Input

Last month we developed and refined your long-term vision for your company. Now that you've been building trust and fostering the motivation of your employees, it's time to get their input on your vision.

Create a plan for getting honest feedback on how they see things going, as well as their ideas for strategies, changes, opportunities that would achieve your goals.

Remember, you are in charge of the vision. You want to ensure that you are asking for their input, not to make the decisions for you. Ensure a clear channel for their input, so they don't run wild and you don't get overwhelmed by dozens of good idea fairies taking up your time.

Also, every time you get a suggestion, be sure to say thank you, and clearly and respectfully explain why you choose not to take their plan. You want to make sure they feel their honesty is still valued, even if their ideas aren't realistic or don't mesh with your vision.

Your plan could be adding strategizing to the regular team meeting, or you could create a system for receiving their ideas and feedback in writing. Whichever way you go, you want to keep the structure clear and focused, and make sure to make the most efficient use of everyone's time.

For example, say it is June and you want to get ready for the holiday sales season to start in September. You might decide to call a strategy meeting outside of your regular time. Set a firm time limit to the meeting and stick to it. You might create a document that analyzes the strengths and weaknesses of last year's plan, briefly describes the goals for this season. The document might remind them of the limitations of time, money, and other resources.

You might ask your staff to come to the meeting with 2-3 suggestions that they submit to you the day before. That keeps you in charge of the meeting, because you can choose to only discuss the ones that you think are viable.

Perhaps from all the ideas submitted, you organize the meeting around how to implement the 2-3 ideas you think are best. Perhaps you need to organize the meeting as a brainstorming session, because your staff does better at being creative by talking it out together, rather than reflecting on their own time. Having that understanding of how your team works best is why you are the visionary and an inspiring example of leadership.

Based on your understanding of how you and your staff are their most creative, create the agenda for your meeting. Schedule it. Schedule time for the prep work you need to do.

Be sure on your meeting agenda that at the end you have time for everyone to state what their next task is as well as a deadline. You might consider delegating keeping written track of everyone's tasks and deadlines to a trusted member of your staff who has demonstrated they are ready for more leadership responsibility.

If you don't have time to accomplish all of this today, find time on your calendar to come back to this. Include it in your weekly focus meeting, as well as reflecting on how you can create a system for regular strategizing with your staff.

Thursday: Maintaining Rapport with Individual Employees

In addition to meeting as a group, you also need to stay on top of regular 1-1 time with your staff. This should be a blend of getting to know them as people and whatever is needed to get them to want to excel at their job. This could be informal training, it could be regular check-ins on their tasks and projects, it could be making them feel comfortable to ask questions, etc.

This rapport allows you to naturally reinforce the core values of your business. It's a great place to make simple references to your core values in regards to whatever comes up in conversation. Having the core values as the cornerstone leads to positive improvements in communication and a sense of excellence throughout your entire business.

Remember, you don't want to only give the grease to the squeaky wheels. Your middle-to-best employees should really get the most of your time. It's more efficient to inspire and develop them. It is an ongoing skill for you to develop: coming to understand how to draw out the best in your people in the most efficient way.

Take a moment to reflect on your habits of chatting individually with your employees. Are you rushed? Controlling? Do you set the tension and busy-ness aside to ensure they have your full attention? Do you end up going weeks at a time without inspecting what you expect in this more 'informal' setting? Do you hold rigidly to preconceived notions of their personality or character?

What are 1-2 small improvements you can make to your communication 1-1 with staff?

Friday: Long-term Vision for Saff Development

There is way more about running meetings and strategizing with staff than can be covered in one week. My goal is to get you moving toward more efficient systems of communication so that you can leverage the strengths of your staff.

Pull out your 6-month and 1-year goals for your company. Is staff development on the list? Either take some time now, or block off time on your calendar to come up with your vision for how to incorporate staff development into the plan for your company.

Things you'll want to consider include

o   Am I continuing to develop my skills as an effective and respectful communicator with my staff?
o   Do I have a regular time to reflect on how efficient and useful my meetings are? How often do I need to reflect and strategize running meetings more efficiently?
o   How can I continue to improve my systems for delegating, running meetings, and encouraging my staff to take more responsibility for the success of my company?

o How can I better create opportunities for my staff to develop their own skills? What rewards or systems need to be in place for that?

When I have an excellent employee, I develop them. I let them know opportunities for growth within the company that are in the works. They become highly motivated and help the business succeed in its goals because they get to reach new heights in their careers. As your business grows, the best of your staff should get chances to benefit, they should know opportunities are out there and exactly what they need to do to seize the opportunity.

WEEK 4
HIRING AND PROFESSIONALISM

Monday: Hiring as a Small Business

Training a new employee is expensive and time-consuming. You don't want to invest that any more than you have to, so plan to hire for the long-term. There need to be opportunities for excellent people to grow with the business as I mentioned.

For the most part, I hire from within my network. My first employee was actually a client of mine. She's still with the company, 8 years later. It is a lot easier to know someone's character and capabilities if you already know them, or if someone you respect vouches for them. My best staff will often come to me with someone they know that they think would be a good fit.

Even if you hire minimum wage teenagers, you still want to do the best you can to ensure they align with your core values. Incorporating core values into the interview process makes determining if they are a good fit very straightforward. It also shows them right out the gate what is expected of them.

I base all my interview questions off my list of core values. I will ask interviewees to define several of the core values and describe a time they witnessed or demonstrated them. I ask at the end if they feel they can come to work every day and embody the core values. It's a great way to show from the beginning the expectations you have, and it gives you a chance to assess the honesty of their response.

There are all kinds of techniques out there for conducting interviews. Your job as the visionary is to be willing to experiment and keep testing things until you find the technique that is the exact right fit for you.

Most of the skill of interviewing is being a genuine person, being real about what the job entails, and taking the time to listen and observe carefully. The more relaxed you are, the more relaxed they are, and the better you can assess whether or not you two will mesh well, and that they will mesh with the systems of your business.

Remember, employees are like a second family. A lot of people spend more time with their coworker family than their blood family. That is a deep relationship! You are all pulling together to succeed and grow as people. It's as much about whether or not you and your new employee can get along, be honest, be respectful, follow the core values as skills or abilities on their part.

Tuesday: Dress Code

A dress code might not show up in your core values, but if your employees interact with the public, it is essential that they look the part.

Think about a police officer. Think about how the uniform, the badge, commands instant respect and understanding of their duties when they walk into a room in that uniform.

Ensure your staff dresses so that customers and clients have an instant understanding of what to expect when they see that staff member. You want that instant understanding of what to expect to be an expectation of excellence.

In this day and age, authoritative leadership is countercultural and a dress code is associated with authoritarianism. While you don't want to be so heavy-handed you lose respect when you convey your dress code expectations, you want to be firm and clear.

Here is another instance where core values, expectations, and explaining why it's important make ensuring your business fits your vision so much easier and more efficient. If staff know why you have certain expectations with dress code, then they're less resistant. If staff know that you inspect what you expect, they know that if they come to work in that sloppy shirt then you are going to notice and say something, and they are going to make the right choice.

First, start with your own attire. Do you dress like the successful, talented business owner that you are?

Second, think about your staff. Do you need to implement a dress code? Do you need to outline your expectations and then inspect what you expect?

Create a plan for increasing the professionalism and quality of appearances amongst yourself and your staff. Remember, make the change manageable and sustainable.

Wednesday: Reward Excellence

I've already mentioned this, but I want to be sure you fully incorporate this into your systems for working with staff.

First, any time someone does something excellent, praise them publicly. Let everyone know you noticed. This should be done both formally in meetings or emails, and informally. It is also a good practice to iterate the praise in 1-1 interactions.

Second, make sure staff have a clear understanding of how they can grow with the company and give them opportunities to feel more invested. For example, I was looking to expand to a new store within a year. I had an employee who was just above and beyond. Once I committed to opening that second store within a year, I arranged a meeting with that employee. I let him know I wanted him to be the store manager when it opened. I then shared with him my plans for marketing the new space and developing a sustained customer base. I invited him to participate in the process. He came back fired up, full of great ideas for advertising, etc.

Look at how you reward excellence currently. Create a plan for a new system for rewarding excellence. Maybe it is adding bonuses, maybe it is a system for how to earn raises, maybe it is paying for a training program or workshop. It depends on your business and your goals and your staff.

Remember, if you need to do research, build new skills, or balance this against your other goals and needs, to take all of that into account in your planning. Use that calendar to automate.

Thursday: Nobody Cares More than You

I cannot emphasize enough that you set the standard with both your actions and the effectiveness of your communication. Your staff is not going to care more about your business than you do. So every time you interact with them, the depth and commitment of your care needs to be present.

If you care about cleanliness, you can't just say it in meetings or write it down as a core value. No, if you care about cleanliness, every time you walk into your store you have to inspect how the place looks and either clean it yourself right then or ask someone to take care of it.

So, do you feel frustrated with any of your employees? For the most part, they take their lead from you. Pick something that frustrates you and create a plan for resolving that frustration. Maybe it's a staff training, maybe it's a 1-1 conversation, maybe it's a change in your actions or your communications.

Friday: Looking Back Over the Month

Based on all the reflection and new strategies and skills you are beginning to develop this month, rate the current level of trust between you and your employees from 1-10.

Building trust isn't just refining how you communicate, it is refining how you listen. Take some quality time to reflect on your communication, in particular how you listen.

Core values inspire excellence and foster communication. They are at their best when they are simple and direct. How is your development of your core values going? What tweaks do you need to make to refine how they are being developed and integrated into your business?

Professionalism is the gold standard of trust and respect. Professionalism starts with you. Do you maintain a sense of excellence? Do you have clear means of using the tools, processes, and goals of your business to inspire your people to greatness?

Automate meetings. When everyone knows what to expect in terms of how a team or 1-1 meeting is going to go, it frees up their mental and emotional energy to be better dedicated to their work.

Which of these have you mastered? Which needs the most emphasis right now? Add the colors and contours to your vision for your business and arrange your time accordingly.

MONTH FOUR
GETTING LEADS IN THE DOOR

A couple years ago, I took my staff of 15 on a walk in New York. I told them to observe the restaurants we passed in order to pick where we would eat for our team lunch.

We walked by almost 20 restaurants before we found somewhere we wanted to eat. That is 20 restaurants that had a chance, and failed to get clients in the door.

The restaurant we walked into was polished, sophisticated. We almost didn't want to eat our meals because the plates were so artfully arranged we wanted to delay the joy of eating for the satisfaction of savoring with our eyes. The presentation—from observing the storefront to that last mouthful—was the epitome of professional.

Why is it that only 1 out of 20 got this group in the door?

Most small business owners don't know how to adopt a learning mindset. When you don't open your mind to being coachable, when you don't open your mind to being humble to admitting that maybe you don't know it all and that you can learn from others' example or insights, then you aren't going to be able to recognize that the reason 15 people paused outside your restaurant and then kept walking down the street is because you are making a mistake.

You can't continue to expand your ability to get clients in the door if you can't learn to recognize your mistakes, or where there are areas for improvement in how you conduct your business. Just because you've always been able to get along doing things the way you've been doing them doesn't mean that's a good reason to keep on with those practices.

WEEK 1
LEAD GENERATION & YOUR STORE FRONT

Monday: Why It Matters

In the 21st century, you can no longer just think of your store front as the physical wall and sign marking the entrance to your store. There are multiple "store fronts" now: the physical building, your website, your Facebook page, and your description/reviews on websites like Yelp or TripAdvisor. Each of them is a window that potential clients are going to glance into to determine whether or not they want to trade their money for your goods or services.

Having this mindset helps you create systems for lead generation and maintaining your value in the eyes of clients, both new ones and those you hope to retain.

Take some time to reflect on your storefronts. Both in terms of what they look like and in terms of your perceptions, beliefs, behavior, and values are around them. Do you have a learning mindset?

Tuesday: Guerrilla Marketing

For the small business owner with a limited marketing budget, guerilla marketing is the way to go. In the first years of running my company, we would print thousands of fliers and distribute them across town. With the advent of social media and the internet, you have to invest more creativity and cover more angles than simply creating and distributing an eye-catching flier as that window-glimpse into your business.

Use the information below create your own spreadsheet, or research a software program you could invest in to track your campaigns. You will want to be able to have a straightforward, objective way to assess the effort of conducting a campaign vs resources invested against the result. And a way to regularly assess and observe changes over time.

- Storefront, physical
- Storefront, online (website, Facebook, Instagram, etc)
- Campaign
- Frequency of change
- Clients Attained
- Whose responsible for what
- Date of Strategy/review session
- Staff Hours

Add this to your weekly meeting, or schedule in a time to create the vision for how you will use each store front to create lead gens. We will talk in more detail about other ways to engage clients next week. This week it's about getting practice with the big picture view of how you currently demonstrate your value to clients, and for beginning to get a sense of what you need to research and learn more about.

Wednesday: Prep Your Campaign Vision

The key to guerilla marketing is creativity. That's why it is so important to learn to delegate, and to learn to train your staff to be leaders. If you have begun to take those steps over the past 2 months, you've freed up your time and energy to be creative in your marketing, and you've also begun to motivate your staff to bring their best creative selfs to work for your business.

Take a few minutes to research guerilla marketing campaigns. Take notes on what you might be able to incorporate. You might want to create a digital file or bookmark folder with links, insightful articles, or just graphics of successful ads for the visual stimulation when you are sitting down to put your creative brainstorming hat on.

Don't go running off starting a campaign just yet. Today is just about info-gathering. It's important to let everything simmer, and to return to your big picture goals as well as staff and resource assessment before dedicating resources to a new line of effort.

Thursday: Pause for Research

Master Chhe, my first boss would send me to local seminars to learn about marketing. Because I was young and excited for my path, I was hungry for any and all knowledge. That hunger, and that investment of my time and money into learning from experts, made all the difference in the success of my company.

With the rise of the internet, successful marketing techniques evolve at a faster rate than ever before. Nobody can afford to think they already know it all, especially if you want your business to expand.

Picking someone to learn from requires research and prior planning on your part. Do you feel skillful and at ease with contemporary marketing techniques? Is it easy for you to continue to keep your store front engaging and professional?

Take a moment to jot down a few areas you could stand to learn more about, and develop your skills in.

Now, take a few moments to begin a research file on who you could learn from.

You need to consider,

- o   How much time and money you have to reasonably invest (remember not to skimp this, the ROI of investing in your skills will be worth it)
- o   What kind of learner you are (can you learn from books? A self-paced online course? 1-1 mentoring?)
- o   The difference between 'respecting' someone and 'clicking' with them. Your selected teacher should be one you believe can

truly teach you something, not necessarily someone you like at a personal level.

o   How they give individual feedback.
o   Who else are their students? Do you match the types of students that gravitate to this teacher?
o   Their portfolio.
o   Whether or not they truly have an open mind and a learner's mindset.

First, you get clear on what your learning priorities are. Then assess how much you can reasonably invest. Then, determine what programs best meet those needs and schedule them in.

You'll also want to assess their effectiveness, as well as assess yourself as a learner. As a small business owner, you want to continue to develop your ability to learn.

Friday: Get Creative

How else can you adapt your first impression on leads to encourage them to want to trade dollars for value? Take some time over the weekend to observe and get creative on what else about the flow of these spaces can encourage people to walk in, stay awhile, and have a good time. Add it to a regular assessment to see how you can update your storefronts, so that everything stays fresh.

When we get to later chapters on lead generation and closing sales, you will want to return to your storefront to make sure it is on-brand, and encourages people to join your 'funnel' of promotions, sales, deals, and loyalty programs. Let that start to marinate now as you observe your space and how people interact.

WEEK 2
PROFESSIONALISM

Monday: Why It Matters

Remember in the chapter introduction how we walked by 20 restaurants before finding someplace that appealed to us enough to want to walk inside?

The professional appearance of your various store fronts and staff gives signals to potential clients about the value of your goods or services.

You should have regular dedicated time to cleaning and updating your store.

And regular dedicated time for your website and social media accounts.

Check out chapter 11 for more detail on this if you're ready for it.

Tuesday: Build Updates into Your Calendar

It is going to depend on your business the frequency and level of updates.

Let's start with building in the most important updates into your calendar. Once you've mastered that you can get more sophisticated.

Pull out your calendar and look to the holidays in the next 12 months. Block out time on your calendar for planning and strategizing. Block out time on the calendar of the employees who are going to help you. You might want to calculate whether or not you need them to work extra hours during peak seasons. You don't want to skimp on this to save dollars if it is going to cost you the respect and perspective of value of your clients.

You need to consider how far in advance you need to plan, which takes into account how much time and effort each sale needs. Pull out your earnings around those key dates. When do you start to see an influx of sales? You are going to want to have everything set up and running smoothly a week before the influx, which means you are going to want to plan 2-3 weeks out, so that there is enough time to implement your plan.

Now block out time on your calendar for a time about a week after the key events. You are going to want time to reflect on what worked and what didn't, document everything so you can be more efficient at the process next year.

You need to consider whether or not you need to take more time to research your industry and business tactics to see if you need to learn anything new before your strategy session.

You need to consider your own time management. Are you being too ambitious? Not ambitious enough? As a business visionary you need to have a keen sense of your own tendencies, so you can mitigate the ones that prevent you from expanding your success.

Wednesday: Go the Extra Mile with Professional Appearance

Now it is time to consider your dress code, bathrooms, entryways, and signage. Before you begin your work day, take a few minutes to honestly and minutely examine each of these. At this point you should be skilled enough to make a quick and honest assessment of what needs improvement to enhance the professional appearance of your business.

Pull out your shorthand summary of your main goals and resources. Where can you block off time, money, or resources to make improvements to these areas, based on the needs of your business? Add it to your long-term strategy.

Thursday: Professional Appearance Online

Now it is time to consider your website and social media.

Is this at the bottom of your priority list for the professional appearance of your business? If so, that needs to change. Online presence is only going to become more important to your clients' perspective of your value.

Take a moment to honestly appraise your website and social media presence.

Write down 3 areas for improvement.

Pick the one that is most pressing, and create a strategy for turning the situation around. What resources do you have on hand that you can leverage? Do you need to learn more skills or delegate? Where is your time and energy best directed in enhancing the value of your online presence?

Friday: Strategize, Plan, Implement

Now that you've adjusted your vision to account for prioritizing the professional demeanor of your store, website and social media presence, can you translate that vision to your staff so that they are inspired to be leaders in this domain? Look back through the month on staff, and take a few minutes this morning for drafting a plan for enhancing your staff's ability to care about professionalism. Remember, they take their cues on what to care about from you.

If you don't have staff, see what you can delegate, and find ways to stay on top of regular polish of your first impression without getting bogged down. Later months have big projects and lots of new skills, right now needs to be about getting really efficient and freeing up time for learning and implementing new processes later on.

WEEK 3
BUILDING TRUST

Monday: Why It Matters

The professional appearance of your physical and online store fronts, and the value promised in your lead generation should be geared to build trust with your clients. When they trust you to provide quality services or goods that are consistent with their impression of your business, they are going to be more willing to engage in trading value (their dollars) for value (your products/services).

Building trust is a crucial component of lead generation. Customers need to trust that you are offering goods/services in good faith, that your deals are mutually beneficial, and that you are not out to cheat them in any way.

The more your clients trust you, the more likely they will be interested in your upsells, future deals, becoming regulars, and spreading the word about the quality of their experience with your business.

If your Facebook page/website don't have up-to-date hours or prices, you have set yourself up to be distrusted before the client has stepped in the door. If your store is dirty, or your staff surly, clients are going to distrust the worth of your goods/services.

If you are short-tempered, distracted, or otherwise self- involved when interacting with staff, customers, or others in your network, you are inviting distrust.

Trust is hard to quantify, but it is essential to the process of engaging with those potentially interested in conducting transactions with your business.

Tuesday: Reflect and Check-In

Looking back over the professionalism content from last week, do you need to increase anything as a priority?

Looking over your staff training and evaluations, come up with a strategy for instilling them with a better sense of building trust. Is this training something you can delegate to an exceptional staff member? How will you reward them?

Take a moment to think about your interactions with customers. What about your professional demeanor would you like to improve? Who in your network can help you with that? You are going to want an outside opinion to help you give a realistic evaluation.

After spending a little bit of time thinking about these things right now, create a few lines on your agenda for your next week's planning session.

Wednesday: Focus your Brand and Mission

Now it's time to talk about trust in your marketing strategies. Pull open your 'About' page on your Facebook, your 'About' page on your website, and any other descriptions of your brand/business that you have, either private or public documents.

Take a moment to read them over. Write down all of the promises you make to your customers.

Take a moment to revise these to be more powerful. If this isn't a skill you have honed, add a line to your weekly agenda to troubleshoot this. Do you need to develop this skill, or find someone to delegate to? What resources will be required?

Are the messages simple, straight-forward, and emotionally compelling? Are they coherent? Do you have too many? Too few?

Now that you've begun to develop systems for updating your professionalism, do the steps you've made in that direction offer promises to the customer that are in alignment with your written (and verbal) promises to customers?

Pull out your notes on staff training and marketing campaigns you've conducted in the past. Take a moment to start reflecting on whether or not your training and campaigns align with the promises you make to customers in your 'store fronts'.

Let all this simmer in your brain today and while you sleep. We'll pick this back up tomorrow and Friday.

Thursday: Build Authenticity into Your Brand

People trust authenticity. Being authentic is a skill and approach that you and your staff can develop.

There are many techniques for developing and conveying authenticity. It starts with a firm awareness of the promises you make to customers.

There are many other strategies for instilling a sense of authenticity into your business. Some examples include:

- o Adding personal touches. This could be taking a few moments to interact with customers, it could be in the language of your emails or website, or how you handle your social media.
- o Fostering and sharing positive reviews of your business. People trust customer reviews. These can be shared on your website or in your store. You can also enact strategies for strengthening your reviews on sites like Facebook, TripAdvisor, Yelp, etc.
- o Demonstrating a sense of social responsibility. More and more, people care about the ethical and moral impact of their purchasing choices.

o   Active and compelling resolution of customer complaints. When people can see that you address and resolve customer complaints in a positive way, they are going to see you as authentic.

Take a moment to evaluate your effectiveness in all four examples. You might want to take the time to research other ways to demonstrate authenticity. Tomorrow, we will strategize based off your observations. It's important to take the time to carefully observe, analyze, and think through how things are currently, before switching to creating and implementing changes. Taking that time means the changes are going to be more meaningful and sustainable.

Friday: Authentic, Trustworthy Brands Have Marketing Campaigns, Too

Fostering a sense of authenticity needs to be a major priority in your business, and something that is considered when developing marketing tactics or making any other changes to your business. One of the biggest keys is consistency, and that is why it is so important to develop strategies for every aspect of your business, and to continue to automate those strategies and make them more efficient.

Having an open mind and an attitude of learning is another key aspect of developing the authenticity of your business.

People who are humble and able to easily admit their ignorance in order to learn and get better are perceived as highly authentic.

Before we get to developing other strategies, let's start with you. It would be more beneficial and effective to find a trusted person with the right expertise to observe and evaluate your interactions with customers. But now might not be the right time for you to invest the time and resources into that evaluation. What you can do is observe your own behaviors toward clients and come up with new goals for interaction.

As you go through your day today, observe your interactions with customers and the thoughts that run through your head. Are you exhausted, resentful, distracted, overwhelmed? When you are listening to customers, are you thinking about other thinks instead of focusing fully on them as they talk? Are you genuinely cheerful, or is it forced? Do you get regular, consistent sleep and nutritious, regular meals? Pick one of the three, and develop a strategy for resolving it.

Now, to the marketing side. Which of the 4 examples from yesterday is the most reasonable for you to invest time/resources into improving right now? Write down your evaluation of the benefit of investing in improving that domain.

Write down your current process.

What are some sustainable changes that you can implement and automate? What will be required to make that happen? What is the time investment? How can you use calendars, your daily/weekly agenda, your staff training, etc, to automate this process with just the right amount of effort? Develop your plan now, or block off time to do it in the next few days.

WEEK 4
BEGINNING TO AUTOMATE MARKETING AND SALES

Monday: Why It Matters

We all know that in the information age, the world has sped up. We create information at an unprecedented rate, and we all swim in a vast sea of information every day.

What this means to you as the master of the game of drawing attention to your business is learning to think of marketing differently.

If you want your business to expand, you need to be expanding the number of trades between you and customers, be they returning, new, or being upsold. That means expanding the effectiveness and reach of your marketing techniques.

This is where automation becomes crucial. Hopefully, practicing automation in the previous 11 weeks means you have developed the skill enough to implement automating systems in your marketing practices.

Machine guns are rapid-fire, quickly dispersing a lot of bullets across a broad space.

If you aren't as skilled at marketing, or are hesitant to learn new techniques, this is going to feel a little overwhelming at first, but since you've developed your employees, your time management, and the professional appearance of your business, and have a new understanding of the value of building trust and being authentic, I believe you can handle it.

Tuesday: Have a system for tracking leads—CRM Software

Let's start with how you are tracking where your leads come from. It's going to be more efficient to have a tracking system from the beginning than to try to implement one in the middle of increasing the speed and reach of your marketing.

If you aren't tracking how leads are coming in, you have no way to evaluate the effectiveness of your marketing tactics.

Take 15 minutes to research customer tracking softwares.

Take another few minutes to shoot a couple emails to other business owners whom you respect (ideally in a similar industry to you) and ask them what software they use and what the pros and cons are. Write your notes in your journal.

Next, add making a decision on what tracking system to use into your agenda, you can flip ahead to month 7, week 1, or you can put this on the radar of your calendar for 3 months from now. You're also going to need to block off time, not only for research, but also to make sure you are thoroughly trained, and that your staff also gets thoroughly trained.

Wednesday: First steps in building software automation

Now it is time to start becoming more efficient and skillful at using multiple types of marketing all at once.
- Fliers, email, Facebook,
- Text messaging,
- Internal promotions (market to own clients), Gift certificates,
- Referral program, Loyalty program, Social media presence,
- Presence in other online spaces, i.e., Google listings, yelp, etc Collaborative projects with other businesses,
- Plus other creative ways to get your business noticed.

Circle the ones you already use. Are your systems for those already automated? Are they tied to the yearly calendar and your sales seasons?

Are they brand consistent? Do you have methods in place for evaluating their effectiveness?

Either take the time now, or block off time in your schedule to evaluate how effective and efficient those systems are. There is almost always room for improvement, so see if you can use what we've learned so far to come up with some simple strategies for making your current marketing tactics more effective (i.e., maybe it is time to invest in a quality graphics designer for some new graphics for your fliers. Maybe it is time to come up with a quick template for fliers that is easy to update for each sale. Maybe it is time to update where and how often you distribute fliers).

We dive deep into these concepts in later chapters, but I want you to start observing and becoming aware of the systems you currently use, so that you are ready to pivot when we cover these points more in depth in the second half of the book.

Thursday: Learn and implement new marketing techniques

Looking back over the list of different forms of marketing, pick 2 that make the most sense for you to begin to include in your business. You might choose based on who your target market is, easefulness of incorporating, cost, current skills and resources, etc.

Remember, the eventual goal is to be able to easily use almost all the types of marketing almost all the time, with minimum effort, and maximum result.

Now, break down the project into smaller pieces. What software, skills, resources, and knowledge are required?

For example, say you want to start having regular email campaigns leading up to major sales events.

Do I have the time to write an email every week? Can I delegate?

Do I have the skill to write an email every week? Can I learn? How much time will it take to learn? How will I learn?

Do I have an archive system for keeping emails for re-use later on?

What should my email template look like? Both in terms of visual design and what types of content I will have?

What are the measurable goals that I have for implementing an email campaign?

What software is out there that will help me automate sending emails?

How many emails should I have for each sales campaign I want to run this year?

How can I ensure the emails are authentic, professional, personal, and on-brand?

Who is going to handle responses to emails? What systems do I need to set up for that?

What actions will I be encouraging customers to take? Do I need to research tips and tactics from business experts?

It's a lot to think about, but remember, investing the time in having a clear and thorough vision sets you up for long-term success and greater ease and efficiency down the line. And, again, we cover it more in-depth later, but starting the ball rolling now will make things easier as you go on with this work.

Generate your own list of questions for both new marketing techniques now. Let it simmer in your brain and jot down new thoughts over the next couple days. Block out time next week to answer the questions and begin to develop your plan for implementation.

Friday: Reflect, Catch-Up, Stay on Top of Your Time

This has been a really intense month of learning. I hope you are beginning to more clearly see the connection between customer perception of your business and the success of your business. You should also be becoming more skilled in your time management and planning sustainable changes that you are not only more efficiently implementing, but also automating.

Take a few minutes to read through the entire month of material; you are looking to see what you still haven't fully grasped. Once you get the concepts and processes, they are straightforward, but it can take time and effort to fully grasp some of these concepts, especially the ones that require personal self-growth.

We often learn the most from engaging in sincere conversation with people who've already been through the learning process we are currently undergoing. Either reach out to the Small Business Profit Arsenal FB group with your questions, or schedule time for a coffee or lunch with someone whom you respect how they run their business. Come to the conversation eager to learn.

Also, as you look through the past month, make sure everything that is on your schedule/agenda for the next few days, the next week, the next month, etc, is on your schedule/ agenda. At this point, there are a lot of moving parts, and we are only 1/3 of the way through.

MONTH FIVE
CUSTOMER RETENTION

As the visionary, you are in charge of efficiency and keeping your company moving in the right direction. Prioritizing client retention defines the long-term success of your business. An efficient and well-run business keeps customers happy and returning. Client retention and the processes you put in place around that needs to be one of your key indicators of the success of your company that you keep at the top of your priorities list.

All the research points to the inherent value of client retention. It saves you time and money. Strong client retention often makes or breaks a business.

A customer that feels that they received a good value in exchange for their money is going to begin to trust you. As we have talked about, that value encompasses more than just the good or product they exchanged for their money.

It is the professional appearance of your space. It is the sense of passion and dedication of your staff. It is the sense of authenticity of your brand. Those are the fundamentals of client retention. From the work you've done the past 3 months, you can build from there to further develop your company's retention of clients.

The essence of this month can't be boiled down to a checklist. Authenticity and genuine trust and rapport with clients aren't a one-off; they require care and attention and genuine fostering of connection.

But, client retention has some common factors that you can use to assess how things stand and create measurable goals to strategize accomplishing: real relationships, genuine gratitude, working feedback systems, problems are anticipated, customer complaints are actively addressed, and customer needs are anticipated.

WEEK 1
BUILD CLIENT RETENTION INTO YOUR BUSINESS MODEL

Monday: Why It Matters

The 3 essentials of client retention are:

o   Real relationships with clients (both you and your staff)
o   Systems for customers to provide genuine feedback on goods/
o   services
o   Anticipating customer needs

Real Relationships

We've already begun to build authenticity and a sense of genuine enthusiasm and investment from your staff. There is plenty more you can begin to integrate in your systems to foster real relationships. We'll delve further into that this week.

Genuine Customer Feedback

Most of the time, an unhappy customer isn't going to say anything, they are just going to quietly go somewhere else with their business. That means you need to take a genuine and proactive approach to finding out what your customers really think.

Anticipating Customer Needs

We get into this in more detail when we start delving into customer pain points, but one thing you can do right now is take a little time every week to see what, where, when, and how you can anticipate what your customers need and provide it to them before they even think to ask. Staying creative and fresh this is a great way to inspire loyalty and build trust in your brand.

Tuesday: The Right Platforms

For developing real relationships, garnering genuine feedback, and anticipating customer needs, you need to be utilizing the right platforms, both internally (among you and staff), and externally.'

It's more important to use a few platforms well than to be dispersed too widely across multiple platforms.

Internally, it is going to be better to use in-person communication and a software. Email is inefficient for communicating with staff. The other thing to consider is making sure you stay consistent and don't jump across platforms for communicating (i.e., send an email one day, a text another, and a FB message another). It's okay to use multiple platforms, but be consistent in what you are using them for. Also, you are going to want to make sure that praise is regularly delivered in a public space—it is much more effective to deliver praise in front of other workers and customers than it is to do so in private.

Block out some time to research software to use for internal communication. There are many platforms out there that have great programs with a free version. After you've researched and chosen the platform you want to use, schedule time to train yourself and your employees on how you want to use it. Like most other strategies in this book, it requires a high initial investment of your time, but makes you more efficient in the long run.

The best right platform for creating real relationships with clients is always going to be in person, supplemented with other channels. It should be a regular part of your planning to evaluate and improve how you interact with customers, as noted in other chapters.

The other aspect of real relationships is demonstrating sincere gratitude and appreciation for their business. There are many tips and tricks out there, it depends on your business what is going to be effective. What is important to note is making sure it is sincere and demonstrates genuine gratitude and is a personal touch that aligns with your brand and personality. This may require some training actions with your employees.

For generating genuine feedback, of course the first step is earning trust. There are many options for generating genuine feedback: surveys, questionnaires, follow-up calls, as well as informal ones between yourself or staff and clients.

The key to generating genuine feedback is learning to ask the right questions. This is going to be a trial and error process that requires you to evaluate the utility and effectiveness of the questions. No one book can develop your expertise. You are going to have to put time into developing this as a key skill of your role as small business owner. This also means evaluating which medium makes the most sense for gaining genuine feedback from your customers.

Anticipating customer needs comes arises from all of the systems we've discussed so far. A reliable and enthusiastic staff whose trust and respect you've earned is critical to this process.

We covered a lot this week. Create a checklist for what you need to research, skill-build, and train staff on.

Block out time for each of these tasks. Remember, if you wisely invest your time on the front end, you are making huge gains in efficiency and sales on the back end.

Wednesday: There is no 'hacking' genuine relationships

As I've made clear in this month and last month, authenticity and trust are essential to developing genuine relationships.

Consistency is key. This should be a blend of regular in-person interaction in an informal, ad hoc way, and a more formal, regular method of connecting. Even as we begin to automate customer communication in later months, the relationships can't be hacked.

Start a file with notes and observations on how people relate to your business. What do people regularly say? What other patterns can you observe about these relationships, both from taking their perspective, yours, your staff, and a more 'objective' third-person type look? Take some time today to start crafting a plan for automating observation and reflection on your, and your company's relationships with customers.

Remember, as a small business owner, the way you relate to people comes from the core values of your business, which is a reflection of your best self. Don't allow personal bias or built-up stress to undermine your living example of your core values. Make this part of your regular check in, as often as you deem it necessary.

Thursday: A frictionless experience

In the modern world, with physical and online storefronts, there is a lot more to manage in terms of making it a smooth and enjoyable experience for the customer from start to finish. One way to evaluate the strength of your client retention strategies is identifying where there is friction in the client experience.

Some common friction points include:

o   Unresponsive FB, email, or other social media presence. Unprofessional physical storefront or poorly arranged stock A website that isn't mobile-friendly;
o   A website (or other social media) that is hard or confusing to navigate;
o   Insufficient attention to educating clients to maximize their benefit from the product/service purchased;
o   Unsatisfactory product/service.

Which of these needs your most immediate attention? Do you have systems in place for regularly evaluating and updating these spaces?

Create an action plan for resolving the problem identified.

Create an action plan for regular assessment of friction points in the customer experience.

Friday: Systems Are Responsive, Not Reactive

To foster real relationships and genuine dialogues, it is more important to do a few channels well, than to try to cover too many and get stretched too thin.

Your business dictates which channels are going to make the most sense. This is going to require research, discussion with your staff and those in your network (both mentors and peers), as well as routine and effective evaluation of how your customers interact with your storefronts and systems. Perhaps for your business, you have such killer sales people that they can inspire customers to fill in paper questionnaires at checkout; maybe Facebook messenger is all you need.

You must learn to get ahead of the power curve in terms of garnering the feedback you need from customers. This requires an enthusiastic staff, carefully chosen software/mediums for interaction, and deliberate fostering of trust.

Learning to be responsive and not reactive is as much an art as it is a science. You can read dozens of books; you can develop dozens of systems and processes—but if you aren't taking the time to genuinely learn from systematic observation of your unique business and your unique clients, you are going to end up trapped in reactive mode and losing lifelong customers.

Action is not going to do much good if you aren't coming from a genuine place in your heart about caring about the impact of your product/services on real people. In the hustle and bustle of running a small business, it is easy to lose sight of that. It's also easy to get lost in the weeds of the opinions of just a few people. You have to learn to be fundamentally honest with yourself and set your ego aside in learning to evaluate your own effectiveness at genuinely connecting with your clients.

Reflect on your process. What do you know about your own tendencies? Maybe look back to earlier reflections to see if you can develop some measures or markers for improvement.

WEEK 2
LOYALTY PROGRAMS

Monday: Why It Matters

People love rewards, and they love to feel like they belong to a community. A successful loyalty program creates both positives for your clients.

Remember, a crucial part of any program that is geared for client retention is evaluating their effectiveness on a regular basis and ensuring that any gaps or holes or problems get resolved.

Do you have a loyalty program in place currently? How do you evaluate its effectiveness? How do you measure success?

Take some time to think about what kind of program you might incorporate, or how you could improve yours. Maybe do some research into your industry on the topic.

Tuesday: Referral Programs

One of the most effective loyalty programs you can put in place is a referral program. Whatever other client retention strategies you use, for most businesses you are also going to want to have some kind of referral program.

Before you launch any referral program, you are going to want to make sure you have your tracking process in place, to see what your investment of time/money gains. **You also want to make sure that you**

have a plan for retaining client business after they've tried your product/service for the first time via the referral program.

It depends on your business what is going to be an effective referral program. Here are some key features to keep in mind as you design:

Ease of effort for the customer. How easy can you make it for them to refer your business? Rules should be simple; rewards should be simple to gain.

Value of reward for referrer and referee. Most incentives have a value for both parties. You are going to want to make sure you are the right level of generous for the long-term health of your business.

There are many creative options for ensuring your referral program fits your budget.

Promotion of program. You need to ensure the program effectively reaches your target audience of loyal, invested customers.

Promotion of the program should be carefully designed based on your customer base. How do your loyal customers interact with your business? If your loyal customers never check your Facebook or website, then promoting the program online is going to miss the target.

Adjusting and evaluating. There are software programs out there that you can use to analyze referral programs among other loyalty programs. Or you can do it, or you can train an employee to analyze the program. The key take-away here is making sure you've incorporated analysis and adjustment into a regular part of your routine.

A good referral program comes from having a solid understanding of your loyal, enthusiastic clients. What rewards are they interested in? What can you do to make it as easy as possible for them to refer your product/service?

Take a few moments to begin to sketch out your plan for incorporating or updating your referral program.

Wednesday: Automate Inclusion into your Programs

Whatever loyalty programs you are using, you need to automate. This means both internally and with the customer experience. For example, if you have a punch card where for every $100 dollars the client spends they get a $10 coupon, you want to train your staff to automatically hand them a punch card after they've made a purchase. Of course, in this day and age, you are going to be better off with a software and a sophisticated website— especially if online is how most of your customers either discover your store or make purchases.

Automation requires:

o   Staff training. Plan to update how you train your staff to incorporate your loyalty programs into their interaction with customers—remember authenticity and building trust are key.

o   Awareness of who your customers are, what they value, and how they interact with your business.

o   Analytics. You must make it a regular part of your process to analyze your programs, troubleshoot, and increase the effectiveness of your programs.

o   Making it as easy as possible for your loyal, enthusiastic customers to participate and to enjoy participating.

o   If you have loyalty/referral programs, which of the above bullets is your current biggest priority for improvement?

Schedule it in.

If you have neither, schedule time to begin to develop your programs, keeping these in mind. If you need to devote time to research, schedule it in.

Thursday: Membership levels & naming your programs

Sometimes, it can be useful to have more than 1 tier to your loyalty program. This creates extra incentive for your most passionate customers. Upon reflecting on your business, is this going to be useful?

If you are still in the process of getting your loyalty/referral programs off the ground, take a moment to envision how you can structure your system to eventually have multiple tiers.

Another key consideration is what you name your programs/how you refer to your most loyal customers. You are going to want to keep this consistent with your brand and the promise of your company. Schedule time to research/brainstorm.

Remember, the names are going to be the first thing your customer sees about the program, and the name you give to your group of loyal customers is going to be part of their positive association with your company. And hopefully at this point you are already considering authenticity as part of your strategy on naming your programs.

Maybe naming is something you delegate—either to a talented staff member or someone in your network. Take a few moments to sketch out your plan for coming up with the best possible names for your loyalty/referral/membership programs.

Friday: Evaluating your program's effectiveness

Your effort at creating these programs means little if you don't have a solid process for evaluating the effectiveness of the programs, and for regular refinement.

Is evaluation something you struggle to schedule in?

Maybe it's time to invest in a software.

Maybe it's time to tap the expertise of a mentor or someone who is succeeding in evaluating their client retention initiatives.

Maybe it's time to come up with a better calendar system for managing your time.

Maybe it's time to delegate to a strong employee. Maybe it's time you learn some new skills.

Which is it? Take a few minutes to sketch out a plan. Again, client retention is the most efficient and cost-effective way to generate sales for your company. You have to be paying attention to what works and doesn't work.

WEEK 3
REACH OUT WHEN PEOPLE ARE UNHAPPY

Monday: Why It Matters

Negative feedback is a wealth of information for your business. Just remember that most negative feedback is going to be the silent type— people quietly never returning to your business, or walking by your storefront or clicking out of your website.

If you always reach out to clients when they are not fully satisfied with their purchase, you are demonstrating a level of care and a sense of excellence that only adds value to your company.

But remember—it's not just about appeasing the complaining customer— it's about using that feedback to make long-term improvements to how you do business.

Tuesday: Remember, It All Comes Back to Trust

I've been saying this a lot for several weeks now. Trust is one of your most precious resources. The more you invest in gaining your employees' trust and respect, the more that pays dividends with customers. And the more you carefully attend to fostering the trust of customers through the other methods we've talked about, the more likely you are to hear about any issues your customers are dealing with.

Trust is built and maintained through:

o   Dedicated employees

o Clear and easy channels for resolving issues

o Automated follow-up on purchases

o Fostering personal relationships with customers

If staff aren't happy, customers aren't going to trust them with their issues. If you never respond to emails or don't have a page on your website dedicated to complaints/questions/issues, customers are going to feel frustrated and less trusting. If you don't follow up on purchases to check how things are going, you are missing valuable feedback and an opportunity to foster relationships. If you aren't fostering personal relationships, you aren't demonstrating authenticity.

Which one of these most needs troubleshooting? Where can you take a process or part of your structure and either improve it, or automate it? Schedule it in.

Wednesday: When Customers Complain, Solve for the Root Problem

When your customers complain, it is not just about addressing the immediate complaint. You also have to solve for the root problem and use it as an opportunity to prevent future complaints.

If the complaint is about a product or service, you are going to need to ensure standardized higher quality.

Most of the complaints you are likely to get should be resolved by attending to the lessons in the previous months. And, you can't kowtow to every complaint—sometimes people complain just out of a sense of personal preference and it isn't really going to be worth your time to change anything.

What I want you to take away from here is that you can't just address the complaint and move on. You should be tracking complaints in some kind of database or software, you should be following up with those customers to see how they are doing, you should be ensuring you aren't bending over backwards but are still demonstrating a commitment to excellence, and you should be evaluating complaints to see where the root of the problem is, and how you can quickly and efficiently update your systems to ensure nobody complains about that thing again.

How do you currently handle complaints? Do you log them? Do you dedicate time/resources to identifying what the underlying issue is and resolving it?

Evaluate your current process for reconciling complaints. What can you do to make things better? Can you be more timely in your responses? Can you instill more authenticity? Can you better measure the success of how you address the complaints and make sustainable, real changes to how you do business?

Thursday: Deliberate Targeting of Customer Feedback

This can be handled in many ways. Maybe you have a good rapport with a majority of your most loyal clients—then maybe it is more effective to ask them deliberate questions in informal conversations. Maybe most of your customers visit your Facebook page regularly and a poll is the most effective way to get feedback.

Remember, your customers time is valuable, and your questions need to reflect that. If you are coming from a place of sincerity and genuine desire to improve their experience, you've already won half the battle in your deliberate targeting of customer feedback.

Again, like everything else this month, the strategies you use are going to depend on your clients, and are going to require troubleshooting over time to optimize.

Strategies include: post-experience surveys; email follow-ups; informal discussion; Facebook polls; website pages; rewards for longer surveys.

You are going to want to take time to craft good questions. Scaled questions or yes/no questions are easier to measure, but might not get you enough information. Open-ended questions can give you a greater wealth of information, but are more time- consuming, and are more easily misinterpreted.

Don't ask for people to fill anything out if you aren't going to use the information. And when you use the information, make it prominent—make people feel proud to have contributed to a positive change to your business.

Friday: Big Picture Check-In

How are you doing at automating your schedule and minimizing the time spent on tasks that don't really get you toward your goals?

How are your weekly focus meetings going? Are they helping you set up for the week ahead, and making sure the week moves you toward your quarterly targets, that move you toward your concrete 1 and 3 year goals?

Are you staying creative and positive when it comes to troubleshooting how and when and why you aren't hitting your weekly goals?

Are you staying on top of your physical health? Do you still have your big reason for gaining free time from making all these changes?

Flip back through your notebook, your calendar, and this book. What is working really, really well? Take time to honor that before turning to diagnosing where you can make changes.

Are you still sticking to the principle 'manageable chunks of change?'

The principle of automating your time on a daily and weekly basis?

Do you feel that you are improving at that balance between the big-picture vision and the day-to-day tasks?

WEEK 4
CUSTOMER REVIEWS

Monday: Why It Matters

People use the internet to help them make purchasing decisions. People research reviews before trying a new product or service. In addition to loyalty programs, you are going to want to dedicate time and resources to maintaining your reputation through reviews. Reviews are also a wealth of information about what people think about your business.

Personal stories from customers also garner trust. If your website, physical store, emails/other electronic communication, and social media do not have personal stories of your clients' experiences, you are missing out on a key way to demonstrate the value of your business.

Tuesday: Take the Time to Gather Client Experiences

Pick 5 customers that you know love your product/service. If you can, ask them personally to write a brief review for you to share with others. Put those reviews where they will be to best effect for your business— that may be in your store, your website, a newsletter/blog, or on social media. When you get the reviews, make sure they are shared in a creative and exciting way.

Schedule it in. If you can, ask them today.

Wednesday: Active & Responsive Social Media Presence

People love to post about their experiences on social media. Having an active and responsive social media presence encourages them to share. If you have a Facebook, you should be encouraging customers to post on your site. Hashtags are an excellent resource. Any time someone writes something that positively recognizes your business, you should have a positive and personalized response.

Maybe right now this is something you need to dedicate your time to, but you should have a plan for delegating this responsibility if at all possible. You don't want this to become a time-suck. Scheduling 15 minutes a day should be all you need.

You can't be passive and wait for reviews. Your sales and promotions, holidays, special events, etc, should be actively and enthusiastically shared via social media. The more active your social media presence, the more customers will follow your lead.

If you don't currently have a strong social media presence, take a few moments to begin to develop a strategy for incorporating this into your business model. Remember, delegating to staff is going to make the world of difference. What training and oversight will they need?

Thursday: Encourage Positive Reviews

For the small business, the personal touch makes all the difference. As you find yourself in rapport-building conversations with clients, make genuine and specific requests for them to share their experience—and remember to direct them to the site you want them to write the review on, be it Yelp, Facebook, TripAdvisor, etc. You are going to want to train your staff to do the same. Remember—authenticity is key.

You can also create incentives for positive reviews. Make sure this is a net gain to your business, and make sure to evaluate and optimize any incentives. Consider the seasons and who your customers are when creating a strategy for rewarding positive reviews.

You also want to make sure to keep a database of reviews that you can use as an ongoing resource.

Friday: Tying the Month Together

Client retention is the heart of any successful business. If you don't have a strong and growing core of returning clients, you aren't operating efficiently, and you aren't properly investing your time and effort.

The core of successful client retention is offering a product or service of real and genuine value to your customers. Enhancing the value of your product/services should be a regular part of your efforts as the visionary, and following a 3 to 5 year plan for growth. If you haven't updated or evaluated your products/ services, or thought about the new things you can offer clients, you need to begin there.

Once you have a solid structure of offering real value, you have a foundation upon which to build your loyalty programs, referral programs, and other incentives for returning to the store.

The essential ingredients are creativity, personalization, and authenticity. You need to take regular time to brainstorm and research the market to come up with new and creative ways to connect with customers such that they are motivated to return time and again. You need to ensure that customers feel a sense of personal connection to your business. You need to ensure that you stay authentic and deserving of customer trust.

Pull out your year/3-year calendar. Based on the ebb and flow of your business, when are the best times of year to step back and make those big picture evaluations? Schedule it in. Make sure it is as easy as possible for you to step back and look at the big picture. What resources do you need? How much time on your calendar? Who else needs to be part of the process?

What aspects of your business are you going to analyze—both successes and failures? Gather everything, or make note of everything you'll need, so that when you are doing your big picture visioning around client retention that you are going to be set up for success.

MONTH SIX
BUILD YOUR NETWORK

If you aren't circulating—both in person and electronically—amongst new people, then you are not building brand awareness. Dedicated time to building and sustaining a network gets eyeballs on your brand, and ears tuned in. Systematizing how you grow and interact with people will accelerate your business. You can't just sit in your store and wait for people to show up. You can't focus only on administrative details and on product or service. As the leader of your company, you lead the way for new people to discover and appreciate what you have to offer.

Networking must be deliberate and purposeful. It must be a carefully thought out aspect of your larger vision. As the leader of your company, this is not usually going to be something you can delegate. Your time is one of the most valuable resources of your company, you need to spend it wisely. If networking is not something you currently spend consistent time on, as part of your plan for this month, you are going to need to go back through the previous months and figure out what you can be more efficient at (aka, automate), and what you can hand off.

Ideally, from upping your game with client retention, planning, staff, and the other changes you've been making, you should have more time freed for networking and planning. If you aren't finding that to be the case, go back through the previous months and get the work done. You can't cut corners on planning. When you invest time and energy wisely into planning, you get big returns in all other aspects of your business. It just means getting over that hurdle of making and automating that investment into planning.

We will talk about networking from several perspectives. While I start to introduce marketing techniques, much of that will get covered in chapters 7-9. I'll remind you in those chapter to flip back to this one. Remember, you can read through this book multiple times. The idea is to only start to incorporate as much change as is manageable; test what works; learn from failure; automate successes; rinse and repeat.

WEEK 1
WHO DO YOU KNOW?

Monday: Why It Matters

When networking, you want to start with who you know. But—

Before we get to that, we need to take the time to develop your strategy. Which means having a clear understanding of your central purpose for networking. (And this is something you are going to want to re-visit at your yearly or quarterly planning session). So, based on what your business needs right now to get it closer to your 3-year goals, what is your central purpose for networking?

Is it—

- To have a pool of peers to trade skills, resources, and/or knowledge?
- To find some key business mentors to learn needed skills from?
- That you are ready to position yourself as a leader/expert in your industry?
- That networking is part of motivating your team?
- To build brand awareness?

Take some time to think it over. What you decide is your main purpose is going to guide your strategy and process for some time. You want to make sure you put the time in on clarifying and refining your vision now, so your strategy is the most efficient and effective it can be. Mistakes happen, and you can always course correct, but part of learning to course correct is getting more efficient at the whole visioning process over time.

Once you've developed your strategy, you can think about who you know already, that either fits your goal, or might know someone they can put you in touch with that fits your goal.

Create a list of those people, and develop your plan for investing your time into those relationships. You might want to push starting this part back til next week or so, that way you can use the other skills and knowledge from this month to make the most of those networking connections.

Tuesday: The Elevator Pitch Never Goes Away

I'm sure you've heard about the elevator pitch before. It's ubiquitous. There's a reason that everyone—not just business owners—should develop the skills of the elevator pitch. We already talked about professionalism. Elevator pitches are another facet of that professional appearance that is so essential to gaining trust and conveying a positive impression of your brand and its promise (which, you might consider incorporating elevator pitches as part of your staff development).

Let's start with the basics, then get more sophisticated.

First, the essentials of the elevator pitch content: who you are; what you offer; what problem you solve; who you solve it for; what makes your biz stand out; and, depending on who your audience is, what your ask is (i.e., try our promotion, meet me for coffee so I can pick your brain about x).

We've been practicing being personable, trustworthy, and authentic in our communication. Your elevator pitch is going to have to hit those three notes, plus a few more. Drafting, revising, drafting, getting feedback, practicing, are going to be essential to this process (investing time now pays big dividends later; this pitch is going to be the spark of many a first impression, you want it to light a cheerful fire). Take a few moments to jot down some notes about what belongs in your elevator pitch (refer back to month 4, week 2).

We'll pick this back up tomorrow. You'll be using this pitch— or parts of it—with everyone you mention your business to.

That's a lot of people.

Wednesday: Elevator Pitch Cont'd

Time to cover the sophisticated aspect of your elevator pitch.

The main takeaway here is to make your words and delivery personable.

Personable means that your pitch is emotionally compelling to your audience. This is done through using clear and concise language, reducing jargon, and makes them feel involved, or connected to, the problem you solve.

There is no one formula for making your 20-30 second spiel authentic and personable. Practice and trial and error are your friends. You are going to want to find some trusted people to troubleshoot your elevator pitch with. It is also worth your time to research and study the elevator pitches of the successful.

Take some time to continue to draft your elevator pitch based on what you wrote yesterday, and the goal of connecting to your audience in an authentic and personable way.

Video your pitch and share it on Small Profit Business Arsenal's FB page. Watch at least 2 other people's and give them feedback on what they do well and where they could improve. In the comment below your video, share who your intended audience for this pitch is.

Again, investing time on this now will pay off in the long run. After you've practiced with people you trust, find some low-risk strangers to practice on and observe how they react (without your ego-don't mistake politeness for genuine interest), so that you can test out how successful your elevator pitch is.

Thursday: Leverage Your Neighborhood

An efficient way to take advantage of who you know is to look around to what other businesses or people are in your neighborhood. Take 10 minutes to research who is around you; what local groups might be relevant to you; as well as your chamber of commerce. Local groups in your neighborhood can include networking events, places you can volunteer or donate some of your services/products to; local business groups; as well as other small businesses within your vicinity.

You want to take the time to do a little bit of research to get a sense of what all is out there before you take the plunge into investing your time/energy/resources. It is not about making sure you can get the most bang for your buck, but rather about building genuine relationships that benefit everyone involved. Whatever steps you take to connect to your local community, it needs to be coming from a sincere and genuine place on your part. We'll get more into that later.

Take 10-15 minutes to create a list of 'neighborhood' businesses or groups that might be mutually beneficial for you to reach out to. Take a little more time and write out the strengths and weaknesses of the other organizations; what questions you need to ask before committing to anything; how much time you can invest; and the pros and cons of investing time in each group.

Once you've done your analysis, and taken some time to think it over, then you will be ready to connect. Remember, as a small business owner your time is precious and in high demand.

If you are going to move forward with connecting with other groups, you will be in the public eye, and you are going to want to do everything you can to make sure you maintain people's trust in you, and your business.

Friday: Cross-promotion

Once you have tuned in to who is in your 'neighborhood' that you can connect with in order to achieve your networking goals, then you can begin to think about cross-promotion opportunities. Remember, people aren't interested in gimmicks. This is going to need to be something sincere and creatively collaborative. Also, you are going to want to pick groups or people that are going to be able to follow through on their commitment to cross-promotion (which means you, too, will need to be able to follow through).

If you haven't finished your elevator pitch, block out some time to keep revising it, or practice it and get some feedback.

If you haven't finished researching and thinking about who in your neighborhood or in your contact list you can connect with, block out time to get that done.

If you've done those things, take some time to brainstorm how you could do some cross-promotion with someone in your network you have a solid relationship with. You might do a little research, chat with your cross-promotion partner over coffee, or however it is that you come up with your best creative, visionary ideas. And remember, this cross-promotion idea doesn't have to take place now—if there is a season or holiday that makes the best sense to cross-promote, plan for that. It's your job to have your finger on the future pulse of your business.

WEEK 2
TAPPING OTHERS' STRENGTHS

Monday: Why It Matters

This may seem a little counterintuitive, but in order to best tap other people's strengths, you are going to need to cultivate your listening abilities. If you are self-involved in a conversation, you are going to miss a lot of crucial information and potential opportunities.

The other aspects of tapping into the strength of your network that we are going to cover this week are integrity, professionalism, and authenticity. If you don't cultivate these skills, you are going to waste a lot of time and effort and end up in a lot of dead ends in terms of building genuine rapport and the ability to sustainably utilize the strength of your network.

Remember, networking is about deliberate investment of your time, based on your goals and vision.

Tuesday: Cultivating the Skill of Listening

Like most of the skills in this book, the skill of listening is not a prescriptive list you can just check off and call it done. Listening is an art, and all the bullet lists and advice in the world don't matter much if you aren't deliberately investing yourself in this skill. And, it doesn't matter how good you perceive yourself to be as a listener, it is something you can always improve on. If you have a networking event, make sure you get a good night's sleep and a healthy meal. As we get into later, your physical and emotional health affect your ability to listen and be present with people.

Some common advice is to ask open-ended questions, not to interrupt, not to provide advice or be unduly negative, and to observe your own and other people's body language and facial cues.

Really, the best way to be a better listener is to be open to feedback. You aren't going to be able to improve this skill without trusted outside perspective to help you. My other advice for improving listening skills is to take up a practice that helps develop your mindful attention, such as martial arts, meditation, yoga, etc.

Come up with a plan to get some quality feedback on your listening skills. Developing your ability to listen will not only help you with networking, but also with your staff, your customers, and in your personal life.

Wednesday: The 'Ask'

Many in the industry recommend having an 'ask' at the end of your elevator pitch. It is going to depend on who you are talking to, but as part of tapping the strengths of others, you have to learn how to be consistent, professional, and courteous when you frame and deliver your 'ask'.

Some recommend having an open-ended ask that is a wide-blast delivery (i.e., if you need an estimate for a remodel, mentioning it to everyone, posting it on your personal or professional Facebook account, wide email blast, etc). Others recommend a careful and deliberate ask. It is going to depend on what you are asking for. Any which way you ask, you are going to want to cultivate a sense of genuine gratitude and appreciation for people who take the time to follow through, and you are going to need to make sure you give as much (well, probably more), than you receive.

Make sure you dedicate time to following through on requests from other people. As a small business owner, your word and your follow-through is as precious as resource for your business as your time. Don't overcommit. When you commit to giving more than you receive, your care and commitment will reap dividends for your business over time.

Ask for things that you really need—things that fit with the long-term vision of your company.

Personalize your gratitude for people who take the time to respond to your ask. This could be a small gift, a hand-written note, or a clever and thoughtful email. The key is sincerity and consistency, finding a method and sticking to it.

Looking back over your notes from this month, who can you tap for information; advice; feedback; or assistance? Which of those do you need the most right now? Create a plan for not only asking, but perhaps offering a trade, and for showing your gratitude if they decide to help you out.

Thursday: The Follow Up

Anyone you meet that you have a meaningful conversation with, you are going to want to have a consistent and automated plan for following up. Your best bet is email, LinkedIn, or, for more important connections, a personalized hand-written note. You can develop a few templates to use for different kinds of connections. Do you plan to attend networking events or conferences as a regular practice? Those are going to have different style notes than connecting with mentors or advisors, or with potential clients, or with people you could potentially trade services or collaborate with.

Take a few minutes to think about your overall game plan for networking. What kinds of follow up notes are you going to need?

Every follow up should have a specific and personal remembrance of what you talked about. That can be incorporated into your template. Below are some examples you can use, or base yours off of.

Meeting at a networking event

Hi_____. It was great to meet someone who also values_____. I so appreciated our conversation about_____. I wanted to follow up on our discussion to share notes about dealing with vendors.

Here are mine. I look forward to reading yours. Maybe we can touch base in the next couple months to talk about_____.

Hope you have a great time on that vacation. Take care,

Meeting with a friend of a friend

Hi,_____,

Thank you for taking the time to meet with me yesterday. I can't believe I didn't realize about_____before! It's clear you know a lot about the field. I am going to test out____. Would it be possible to get some feedback from you? I really value your expertise. [one sentence about a specific personal connection]

Take care,

Meeting with a local business you hope to collaborate with in the future

Hi_____,

I am so glad I took the time to drop into your business and see how you run the show. It's clear you've dedicated a lot of time and care into_____. It looks like it is paying off, and I hope it continues to do so in the future.

When I dropped in, we talked about a possible opportunity to____. I know we are both busy, but I think it has real potential. Want to get together for a coffee at the end of the month, catch up, and discuss this idea a little further?

Being in the same neighborhood, we both win when the other wins. Let me know if there is anything I can do to help you out.

take care,

Create a folder within your system for staying organized so that you can have those templates easily on hand as needed. Now the trick is remembering to send them after every connection. One tip would be to add a task of following up to your calendar at the same time you schedule all of your networking events.

Friday: A Comprehensive Game Plan

At the beginning of the month, we talked about having a specific purpose for networking. Ideally, you should be networking in all aspects—to build relationships with customers and leads, to learn from experts, to share and collaborate with peers, and to get help/resources. For this month in this book, we are only focusing on developing one aspect of networking at a time. But—you should have a comprehensive game plan, where, over time, you easily and efficiently incorporate all aspects of networking. Add some visionary thinking time on this topic to your next big picture planning block.

Today I also want to take time to troubleshoot what we've covered so far. What is your weakest aspect of networking? Is it the follow-through (either of seeing an idea to fruition, or of finishing what you said you would do?)? Is it listening? Is it making time on your schedule for networking events?

Is it staying focused with your current main purpose for networking? Is it your elevator pitch? Is it seeking out mentors and being willing to learn? Or something else?

Remember, if you can't honestly admit your weaknesses and be open-minded and willing to change, you aren't going to be able to accelerate your business.

Take a few minutes to observe, analyze and assess your greatest networking weakness. Once you've done that, add it to your weekly agenda to come up with a plan for mitigating that weakness.

WEEK 3
YOUR NETWORK OF CUSTOMERS AND LEADS

Monday: Why It Matters

Gary Vanerchuk explains in his book, *Jab Jab Jab*, the fundamental principle for businesses optimizing their network with leads and customers:

Every action and visual of your brand should be striving to build 'know, like, and trust' with leads and customers. (flip to chapter 9 for more on this concept).

And in order to build know, like, and trust, you need to be giving.

So your fundamental guiding principle for networking with customers and leads should be that. Hone and use your listening skills, shine with your elevator pitch, and demonstrate the authenticity and trustworthiness of your brand with your asks and your follow-throughs. Those all build know, like, and trust.

We will cover more about giving when we get to software automations starting next month. Take some time today to catch up on material so you're ready to focus on these new concepts tomorrow.

Tuesday: Getting to Know your Loyal, Inner Circle

These loyal, committed customers deserve the best of your listening skills. Depending on your business, your memory, and your frequency of contact, you might consider having a note-taking system to help you remember both the personal and professional details of your conversations with customers. Gaining their trust and building rapport with this group of customers is invaluable in terms of helping you troubleshoot your business. When they feel heard, they are going to feel more invested and a deeper sense of belonging.

You might consider hosting some kind of social or networking event that incorporates your loyal customers. When your customers get to know one another on top of you and your staff, they feel a deeper sense of connection. This could be something you collaborate on with some other local businesses.

Also, depending on the kind of contact you have with your customers, you are going to want to develop an efficient system for your customer 'asks' and your customer 'follow-throughs.' If you interact with customers regularly on a personal level, you might consider things like birthday cards, notes of condolence or appreciation, a company 'customer appreciation day,' or other ways to show how you care about them on a personal level. Like everything else, the key is simplicity and consistency.

As with the other facets of your networking, you want to be sure to follow the same tenets of not promising more than you can deliver, being respectful and appreciative of their time and input, and being sure to give back.

The one last thing I want to mention as you build rapport with customers on a personal level, remember that you are a business owner first. If you begin to develop friendships with customers, make sure there are clear boundaries and the personal and professional do not get messily entangled.

Wednesday: Networking for Leads

If you are attending networking events in order to develop leads, there are a few key things to keep in mind.

First, you are going to want to do your research. Take the time to get a sense of what companies will be at the event, and what the companies are about. You might even develop a few of those open-ended questions so you can better implement those good listening skills.

The goal of the research and prep is to ready yourself to find their pain points and set up for a successful follow through after the event. Networking events aren't about closing sales, they aren't about telling everyone everything about what you do. They are about getting a sense of where other companies are at, so that in the future you can make a more compelling (and less desperate) case for why your business meets their needs.

The other goal of research is to begin to prioritize who your real sales leads are. At these events, you want to make the best use of your time, which means a careful balance of being genuinely engaged in key conversations, and making sure to maximize your circulation of the room.

Take a few minutes to research some potential networking events where you could generate either leads or opportunities for leads. Make notes.

Thursday: Incentives for Reviews and Ratings

This is something you are going to want to plan to implement with both customers and fellow business owners.

Create an 'ask' for your loyal customers to write positive reviews of your company.

Start with what medium you want them to do it on. Facebook, Yelp, TripAdvisor, your website, etc.

Then come up with a plan for making it as easy as possible.

Do you ask via an email? On your website? Have a laptop set up at your shop for them to write? Some kind of creative encouragement for check-ins?

Then, come up with a plan for an efficient way to show your gratitude and appreciation. Are you going to comment on every review? A personalized note? A general notice on your Facebook or website? Some kind of discount?

Next, come up with a plan for working with someone in your network to rate each other's businesses.

Friday: Join your Local Chamber of Commerce and Business Improvement District [BID]

Joining your local chamber of commerce and business improvement district [BID] is a great way to get connected in your community, learn about the culture and changes in your community, about the other businesses operating, and to gain free publicity for your business—if you have the right strategy.

I'm currently in the process of opening a boxing club, Juke Box. I'm planning on having that become a chain of clubs for potential investors that want to invest money but not do much handling of operations. Juke Box is great for that type of investor because of how it is systemized.

A couple months before the opening, I went to a BID board meeting. When it was time for me to present myself, I let the local property owners know that I'm going to be opening this new boxing club, geared for adults to have an activity in neighborhood that will keep them strong and healthy. My explanation was well received, and I got asked to share the flier. Board members blasted the flier to their email list of over 10,000 names. So they gave me free publicity because I was part of their network and because I am passionate about what I do, and I am authentic and concise when I share my brand.

That email blast gave me exposure across the city, and so when the grand opening happens, people will be more likely to go because they've heard about me through this trusted channel of communication.

Either take some time today to research your local chamber of commerce and BID, or put it on your weekly focus meeting agenda. They are an excellent source of networking, whatever your current purpose for networking is.

WEEK 4
THE INTERNET & NETWORKING

Monday: Why It Matters

In this era, you need to be networking both in person and via social media. This goes for both networking for leads, and networking with peers and mentors. The essential element is not to get overcommitted and overwhelmed. Take it one piece at a time from where ever you are at, and keep building from there. The more repetitions you get under your belt, the more automated and efficient the process will be.

I recommend using timers to block out your internet networking time. You can get a lot done on the internet in 15 minutes. Make sure everything you do is purposeful, and upholds the values of your brand.

Your online presence with leads and customers should build know, like, and trust by sharing valuable information with the public. For example, an attorney could post on her Facebook page, "Business owners, want to avoid getting sued?," with a link back to her website or a pdf file they could click and download. Her next post could teach them something new, yet related to the topic: what to do when you are actually being sued. The next post in the theme could be how to negotiate with person that has a lawsuit against you.

Think about what's going to happen when they are in need of a lawyer. They're going to go to you because you give solid information. They are going to recommend you to others in their network because you have shown you are knowledgeable. People who follow you are going to consider you to be an expert because you give valuable information.

Tuesday: Social Media Attracts Customers

You need to have a regular social media presence. It can be as intensive or minimal as you like, but it needs to be consistent and authentic. New webpages bump your SEO, and regular online content helps keep you in the minds of your leads and customers—everyone is busy. It's your job to keep shining the light on why your company is awesome and worth their time and money.

Blogs can be a great and simple social media presence. The updates can be simple, quick calendar posts, testomonials, seasonal reminders, pictures, or short videos. You can either create your own, or hire out. The key is consistency and authenticity. Once you get your system set up, blogs really don't take much time, and they can do double-duty as Facebook or Instagram posts.

Another great social media technique is to connect with people who write blogs with strong followings to get featured.

Key to have consistent posting that is engaging. Try to delegate this as much as possible to staff.

Networks rely on know, like, and trust. Having a social media presence that builds these with people is essential to accelerating your business.

The long list of social media platforms can make getting going in this arena feel overwhelming. It's also easy to be cynical about social media and therefore write it off. But, if you are authentic, and if you are systematic, then you guarantee yourself success and growth in your business.

Instagram, Facebook, Twitter, YouTube, and LinkedIn each have their own strengths and weaknesses as well as demographics of users.

It's better to just pick 1-2 to be consistent in and go from there, than have a page on every social media platform but no real presence or freshness of presence on them.

You don't want your social media content to get stale. You want to post on a regular basis. 1x a week is the absolute minimum. You also don't want to have your time get eaten up by social media. If possible, delegate social media to staff. Be sure to train them.

If you are going to head your social media presence for the time being, set time aside 1x a week to plan what you'll post that week. This might be good to incorporate into your weekly focus meeting.

It's best to generate a list of different 'types' of post you can do. I.e., share jokes, repost someone else's content, reminders on sales/upcoming events, shout outs to customers, pictures or info on products/services, etc. Keeping track of how posts fit into the different types is a way to help you keep your content fresh.

However you organize and decide what to share, the key is giving. Give people useful information, deals, the inside scoop, etc.

Another route you can take is having a regular blog, vlog, or podcast that you share on a social media platform. They are a little more time-intensive, but when you give, people notice your generosity and will show their appreciation for it in ways that grow your business. Remember, consistency! If you are going to take this route, block off time in your schedule for brainstorming and drafting.

Don't be intimidated by having to learn new skills. Embrace the discomfort of experimentation and failure. Take a few moments to start sketching out how you will block off your time to get your social media presence up and running. We'll be returning to social media multiple times in later chapters, so you don't have to get everything perfect right now. You just need to get the ball rolling.

Wednesday: Finding your Target Audience Online

Find groups and discussion areas on social media sites where people are asking the questions that your company has the answers to. You can find them on Facebook, LinkedIn, Xing, Twitter, etc. You want to build time in to your schedule to not only monitor, but also participate.

A few months ago, I got on LinkedIn to see what I could find for getting some new insurance coverage. LinkedIn is a great place to network with professionals. I found a group there and made a post saying I was looking for some quotes on car insurance policies. A few people reached out. I connected with one of them in conversation and met with him in person. I asked him to run an estimate on car insurance. He gave me a bid for $1500 per term less than what I had with the other company. At the meeting he said, I also do home insurance. I hadn't mentioned I was looking, but after being impressed with the value I was getting I said, sure, give me an estimate.

So I saved money on car insurance, and I was able to save more on my properties as well. All from one post in the right group. You can do this as the business owner, and you can do this to save money and get great deals in your own life.

Go find 3-4 groups that match your target audience. You might choose to stay on the same platform for ease of use, or branch across multiple platforms to try to catch a wider net. Come up with a plan for spending the right amount of time monitoring and contributing. Set aside a time in a few months from now to evaluate the success of this effort and make adjustments.

Thursday: Online Networking Groups

All kinds of communities and groups exist online in all kinds of spaces. The possibilities for connection are almost infinite. You can join online courses, online chat groups, online communities of all shapes, sizes, and levels of commitment.

You can join groups to learn, to discuss, to share your expertise. You can join groups to mentor, be mentored, meet potential partners for collaboration or cross-promotion, meet people with the skills you need for your home life or professional, and meet potential leads.

For example, I run a Facebook group for small business owners. My intent is to mentor, promote some of my business ventures, create a space for business owners to collaborate and develop their skills, and to develop and monitor a space where members can benefit by agreeing to invite new members in order to get to promote their stuff. Everyone benefits when members agree to be committed to the group by helping grow it.

All of those benefits from just one group that I run!

And these kinds of groups don't have to be a time-suck or distraction, if you've been building the time management skills that have been built in to how I've been teaching you to accelerate your business.

Block out some time to research, brainstorm, or ask people in your network, for some groups to become involved in. Before jumping in and signing up, take the time to research and get a sense of whether or not it is a good fit for you. Knowing what your needs are, what questions you need answered, what discussions you want to participate in, will help you make the right choice.

Spend 15 minutes now doing some research. Then, create a plan for following through. Can you block off 3 15-minute chunks of time a week to catch up in the groups you decide to become a member of?

Friday: Tying It All Together

Networking is a time investment. And especially in the internet age it is easy to get overwhelmed or involved in too many things. That's why having a vision, a purpose, is essential to this process. It's also important to start small, build consistency, and build from there. With networking that involves client outreach, you are going to want to delegate as much as possible to your staff.

Look back over the month. What needs tweaking? What are you having trouble integrating? Go back and find where you are losing momentum and create your plan for catching back up. If you are feeling overwhelmed, break it down to the priorities that match your current needs. At one of your planning meetings, create a 3-month, 6-month, or 1-year plan for growing in this area of your business.

MONTH SEVEN
STAY UP TO SPEED

The world, particularly the marketing world, continues to change rapidly. New technologies and softwares come out every year. There hundreds of people teaching the best ways to market, grow a business, run a business, use software, etc. There is a lot of information out there!

As I hope my stories have been illustrating, I would not have continued to succeed without learning new things. I stayed up to speed, and I stayed consistent. This month we delve into the world of software and online spaces to give you a practical grip on what, where, when, and how, you need to act to stay up to speed.

Making too many changes too fast is as destabilizing as making no changes. Everyone's tolerance for change, everyone's business's tolerance for change is going to be unique. As the visionary, you are responsible for managing the pace and direction of change.

New habits and new pathways in your brain have to get formed. That takes time and patience.

The goal is to make the change so small that it's harder to not do it than do it. Remember Month 1? We've covered a lot of ground on managing sustainable change. Now we turn to radically changing the way you use technology.

I wanted to pause a moment and remind you how you can set yourself up for success with incorporating all this new information, concepts, principles, and techniques to implement.

WEEK 1
LEARN NEW TOOLS TO RUN YOUR BUSINESS

Monday: Developing your Process for Learning New Tech Tools

As the person responsible for every task, every dollar, every item, every action online, it can be overwhelming to think about adding to the to-do list learning new skills and technology.

But in the long run, investing your time to master the technology allows you to have more latitude and space to invest in being creative and generating leads and taking care of your staff. Basically, the more you can hand off tasks to software (and delegate to staff), the more your business will accelerate.

For a while now, various experts have emphasized the importance of having a learner mindset at work. This is even more true for business owners. As I've mentioned before, the number one difference I've seen working with other business owners is how much they are willing to be open to trying new things.

You can't have a growing business without a growth mindset.

And a growth mindset orients toward staying up to speed with the latest trends in marketing, leadership, and technology.

As part of your weekly rhythm, keep time blocked off for mastering the technology you need to succeed. It doesn't have to be a lot of time every week, but putting it on your calendar is how it gets done. From here on out, we will be doing a lot of technology mastering, so if you need more time every day or every week to build these skills, don't sell yourself short.

Recruit people to help you learn. Make sure you make it manageable and stay consistent.

Tuesday: Finding the Right CRM Software

Maybe you've been running your business from your laptop or a paper ledger. Maybe you aren't tracking your customers at all, except to write down their appointment time in your planner, or a smile of "good-bye, thanks for visiting" when they leave your shop.

Sure, it's always worked just fine, and making a big change by researching, learning, and making mistakes and dealing with being frustrated isn't exactly high on your list of priorities. After all, it's worked just fine so far, right?

As we talked about yesterday, and as I've mentioned throughout the book, staying up to speed and accelerating your business means being willing to put the time in on the front end so that you save time and increase your reach on the back end. It's a natural human response to feel overwhelmed, lazy, intimidated, by a big change like adopting a CRM software, or by transferring all your data to a new CRM program. Being a visionary means knowing how to set that human hindbrain to one side and making a rational decision then a clear and doable plan for executing the decision.

The first step to getting and staying up to speed is having a central program that you can use to manage all of the other apps and programs. The one I use is Zapier, and they connect to the largest amount of other apps, but there are many other options for a CRM—SalesForce is a popular and versatile example.

In order to know which CRM to integrate, you need to know how it is meeting your needs. And in order to know how a CRM can help meet your needs, you need to have a thorough understanding of all your business processes.

Where in your processes are you finding the biggest needs for change? Is it closing the sale? Retaining and upselling clients? Is it running marketing campaigns? Is it keeping track of all your sales and customers?

You might also ask someone, or a couple people, in your network what CRM program they use, and see if they will sit down with you at their computer and walk you through their experience with the program.

Narrowing down your priorities for a CRM software is a back- and-forth process. You want to make sure the excitement and pizzazz of the research phase settles before you make your final decision. There are lots of great free options out there, so do not spend more than what is really in your budget. You want to plan to use this CRM for 2-5 years. Being familiar with your CRM software is essential for the work in the following chapters, so you might flip ahead to later chapters as part of your information-gathering phase.

Some considerations for your nonnegotiable priorities for a CRM might include:

o Pricing/value,
o Integration with other apps or programs essential to your business (website included!),
o Enhancing the workflow between the different parts of your business,
o Ability to help solve your current sales, marketing, or customer retention problems

Do not get too caught up in the features lists in your research. You want the program that you and your staff can learn and use. You want the program that integrates with the systems you already use. You want the program that helps you solve for your current sales/marketing/customers/leads problem.

And, I also believe based on my experience in this day and age you want the CRM that integrates with text messaging.

Wednesday: Integrating a Central Program into your Staff

You are going to want to be able to delegate usage of the program to your staff. Now that you've taken a day to think about your options, take time to reflect on how your staff workflow will be affected by the program.

This includes considering how much time/resources you'll need to invest in training. Who will be the second authority on the program after you, and will they need to be rewarded/compensated for the additional responsibility? Who all will need to utilize the program on a regular basis? How do the strengths and weaknesses of your team play a role in using the program and division of labor? How will integration of the new program affect communication and workflow? What potential pitfalls can you foresee? Who can you ask questions about regarding integrating a centralized program into your staff workflow?

Begin to reflect on the questions and write some of your thoughts, observations, questions, and to-dos in your notebook.

Thursday: Making the Decision to Invest in a Program

If you aren't ready to make this decision, take the time to create your plan for what else you need to do to get ready.

Consider what your tendency is. Do you tend to be too hasty, or too hesitant? Can you take this week as an opportunity to refine your growth mindset and develop your ability to refine your internal processes for making decisions?

Your job as visionary is to consider which CRM fits with your priorities, your sales, and how you create and maintain customer relationships. Some are going to have better integration for email campaigns. Some are going to have better analytics. Some are going to have better functionality for internal communication/assigning tasks and projects.

Third, consider how the CRM is organized. Will the way the program runs integrate into how you relate to the numbers?

Fourth, present your short list of options to your staff at a staff meeting. Spend more time listening than talking. You have the final decision, but you can gain a lot of insight and ideas from letting your staff think through the decision.

After doing a 'soft look' at the program and its impact on workflow, it is time to crunch some numbers. How much is the program, how does it fit into the budget, and from your assessment, do you see a strong return value from the investment? Of course in my experience, and in those I've worked with, there has been a strong return value from investing in a program, but if you don't have a full, internal appreciation for this being a sound investment, then it isn't going to be.

Take a hard look at the ROI of investing in the program. Once you are clear, finalize and execute your plan for moving forward with integrating the program into the workflow of your business.

Friday: CRM Should Save your Time so You Can Use It Elsewhere

About 10 years ago I was using a CRM program that kept all the information on a desktop. As we all know, computers crash from time to time. The computer that I owned at the time would crash every few years. Which deleted all of my contacts and information in the CRM program. Thank goodness we still had papers with all the information on it. We had to go back through every single paper contract and re-enter the information for hundreds of clients. And that's not including prospects and leads. It was crazy. But that's what you had to do at the time, and even with all that work, CRM still saved my company time and money because we were using it right. That's how you know you've successfully incorporated CRM into your processes—the system could crash and you'd still be saving time overall to re-enter all the data—not that you want to plan for that!

A few years later, the cloud system came. Now you had the ability to have everything online and backed up on the cloud. So if something ever happened where the software provider if their machines crashed it would still be backed up in the cloud. So now, I don't have to worry about losing my information, with time the tech improved and we have a CRM that is digital and online.

CRM softwares are much more efficient than Excel or Google spreadsheets because of how they integrate with your other systems—especially marketing campaigns and customer retention and upselling. We will be building marketing campaigns in later chapters, which is why it's important to get your CRM now and begin to learn how to navigate it. If you need to flip ahead to other chapters to be sure you are correctly identifying your biggest process problem that CRM can help with, go for it.

WEEK 2
LEAD GENERATION

Monday: Why It Matters

The number one emphasis for staying up to speed is lead generation. Your skillfulness, creativity, and adaptability should always be growing and experimenting in this area of your business. You should always be learning, always talking with other business owners, reading books, and listening to podcasts and reading articles. I know you bought this book, so I know you do take the time to learn, but is there room to refine and improve? Can you stay in a growth mindset when it comes to staying up to speed with lead generation?

Lead generation and the tools you use should take 2 groups into consideration: the people who are already searching for you, and the people who need to be sparked when they stumble upon you. You need to stay up to speed and stay consistent with both groups.

For the people who are already searching for you, we have covered how to do that with maintaining a physical space. You already have a Facebook that you regularly update, and a website with great content. This week we talk about SEO and being searchable on Google. You don't need to become a maestro of keywords, but you need to be aware of the basics, and ensure that you are listening to the words your customers use, as well as ensuring powerful words and phrases show up consistently on your website and other online storefronts.

Look ahead to your schedule, and clear a little more time this week on your schedule to work through the material. Glance over the information in the week ahead and use it to plan your time.

Tuesday: Optimizing for Google Search

First, have you submitted your website to Google's Search Console? If not, take the time to do that right now (some website hosting platforms like Wix will have already done this for you).

The next task, that requires ongoing maintenance that at some point should become automated is having the link to your site in as many places as is reasonable. The link should be on all your social media, and you should have a regular process for inviting and encouraging others to have the link to your site highlighted on their page.

Third, and perhaps the most time-intensive, is learning the new language of keywords, or SEO. If you aren't going to learn it, or ensure a key staff member learns it, then you need to invest in paying an expert to help you tweak the language you use to describe your business on the internet.

Fourth, if your website has a lot of images, you need to both add more text that focuses on the key phrases, and you need to use ALT tags to explain the images and create text for Google to use in its searches.

Ideally, you will take care of all these things, but maybe not today. The key is consistent effort toward your goal, and making sure that you break the tasks down into small,

consistent things you can do every day until your goal of being optimized for Google searchability is accomplished. Pull out your planner or a notebook and create a list of everything that needs to be done to achieve these goals, a time guesstimate for each step (including research and networking), and then build the plan into your schedule for the next month or so.

Wednesday: Getting to the Top of the Local Business Google Search Hierarchy

Ever use Google to find a local restaurant and wonder why something didn't show up?

It's because that restaurant wasn't taking advantage of Google My Business. This is a free feature of the Google search engine that is designed to help local businesses and people using Google Maps to find something nearby. Today, I want you to set the book down and get your business set up on Google My Business (https://www.google.com/business/)

One of the many great features of Google My Business is that you can use their analytics software to gather data on who is searching for you.

Thursday: Getting Listed in Online Directories

There are several other places you want your business listed.

When you are doing this, be sure to consider what information customers are going to be interested in. Hours, customer reviews, and product information are 3 of the top things customers want to know about your business through these online directories. These are also great places to link to coupons or specials, to create that spark for potential customers.

Today, get your business listed on Bing Places for Business, Yahoo Local Listing (they have a basic free option), Yelp, Citysearch (if you are a bar, restaurant, spa, hotel, etc), Foursquare, The Business Journals, Angie's List, and Best of the Web and TripAdvisor if you are willing to invest some cash in a listing with them.

Of course, not all of these might be relevant, and there are other online directories not mentioned here. You are going to need to incorporate upkeep and analytics into your strategic rhythm. This might be a set task for one morning a month; this might be something you hand off. Maybe every 3 months makes more sense for your strategic rhythm. Either way, get that time blocked off and automated on your calendar.

Also, make sure your business info is written the same way in every space, to ensure that the software doesn't think there are 2 businesses.

An Italian restaurant that I know recently changed hands. The website is linked to some other restaurant in another state. The servers and hostesses get phone calls all the time with people placing orders based on the other company's menu.

Their menu is completely different. That's a lot of people getting frustrated right out the gate, often before they've even tried the food! If the owner had a set time for checking in on his online presence, think how much time he'd save his staff, and how he can improve his brand presence in the community.

Friday: Mobile Website Optimization

More and more people use their phones to search for businesses. It is essential that you ensure that your website is optimized for mobile. Part of that is making sure your hours, location, and contact info are easy to find.

Block out some time within the next week to ensure that your site is optimized for mobile.

It is critical to assess the strengths and weaknesses of your website content and organization of pages and links.

Track down what keywords people are using to land on your webpage.

List the 10 most visited sites on your page. What is similar about those pages? Is it the content? Is it the length? The layout? The keywords? The links? Analyze your most visited pages and create a plan for rearranging your site to capitalize on what you've learned.

Some common industry practices include

- o   Headers with keywords/demonstrating they meet the needs/
- o   Pain points of target audience
- o   Short url
- o   A healthy amount of outbound links on each page
- o   A healthy amount of links to other pages on your site
- o   Ensuring image file names have your keywords
- o   Including social media sharing buttons

o   Finding your right balance of length and quality of content

We'll return to website optimization in later chapters. Do what you can right now, focusing your efforts on optimizing your process and your weekly rhythm of work.

WEEK 3
INTERNAL SOFTWARE

Monday: Why It Matters

By now, you should be getting closer to automating how Zapier (or the other program you chose. For ease of reading, I am going to focus on Zapier) functions within your daily and weekly workflow.

This week, we are going to get up to speed with other software to help make your business more efficient, and free up your time for the tasks of the visionary.

First, is getting up to speed with your CRM. The software that tracks your customers and sales. This software helps keep you organized, helps you manage leads and manage re- marketing campaigns, it helps you keep track of delinquencies, and it has a lot of automations built in. In addition to that, it helps you keep track of sales, and get a better sense of the patterns, which helps you plan marketing campaigns and make business-savvy decisions in all areas of your business.

How is your incorporation of your CRM going? Be honest. Reflect about where the kinks are. Have you not given yourself enough time to train? Have you gotten impatient or hasty in building reps in the new process? Are you getting intimidated by all the features? Write it out.

Take a moment to find where the stress or tension is residing in your body. Take 5 minutes to deepen and soften your breath, letting the tension melt away with your exhales (without forcing). If you feel ready, begin to troubleshoot incorporating your CRM now. Otherwise, let it simmer in the backburner of your subconscious, but keep making sure you're draining out the creativity-blocking tension.

Tuesday: Integrate your CRM with your Website

The long-term goal is to have your website be a funnel for lead generation and for translating leads into sales and sales into long-term loyal customers. The goal is to be getting so many people clicking onto your website that your old Excel database system (or paper system, or seat-of-your-pants system) can't handle the amount of data anymore. This increase means that your website and your CRM need to be optimized.

I don't know which CRM you chose, so I can't walk you through that process. Set this book down til tomorrow and go do the legwork for making this optimization happen. If you don't have space in your schedule for it today, make it a priority on your tasks this week.

Wednesday: Integrate your CRM with your Accounting Software

Keeping track of the money flow (and where it's blocked) should be easy and not take a lot of your time. Your time belongs to creatively thinking of ways to bring people in, and to increase and enhance the value of their experience with your company.

Take today and get that CRM integrated or optimized with your accounting software. Start finding those ways to save yourself time with the money flows so that you'll have the time necessary for the months ahead.

Thursday: Refine How Your Team Communicates

Some of the CRM software have internal communication channels. Some have options for widgets, or for interphasing with other programs. Now is a great time to refine how your team communicates.

As we talked about previously, you want the bulk of your praise, instruction, and criticism to be in-person. But, inevitably, we also use email, phone, etc, to communicate with staff and co-workers.

Today and tomorrow, go into observation mode. Take careful, objective notes about how your team communicates. Think about what patterns exist around great communication and poor communication. Is there something that everyone always forgets to do? How do your leaders communicate with other staff?

Combine your observations with your sense of the new CRM program to get a head start on best practices. Once you've done your homework, get a discussion going among your staff. Invite them to come to the next staff meeting with some ideas for how to improve the flow of communication. Be thoughtful and frank, and reserve the right to make the final decision.

Friday: Staying Ahead of your Learning Curve

A few years ago I decided to take a course in social media marketing. I felt pretty good about my skills, but I am always hungry to learn more, so I signed up.

I was blown away by how much I learned from this course. I could not believe I had that much to learn, still!

How I knew I was really learning the material is, I would complete the course module, watch the videos, etc, then I would take what I learned and start applying and testing it in my business. How I really knew I was learning was by how much my business was changing (and gaining more leads and converting more leads to sales) as a result of my applying the information.

I could probably sell my business tomorrow and be wildly successful as a marketer because of how much I learned from applying all this new information and testing it out in my business.

I have a solid process and practice for taking what I learn and applying it. When you don't apply it right away, you just forget it. There's been a lot of new information this month already. A lot of changes.

Let's take a moment to troubleshoot your weekly rhythm, to make sure you're making the most out of your time and balancing between all your tasks.

How is that weekly focus meeting doing, preparing you for the week ahead? Rate your confidence and skillfulness with that.

What small change could you make to improve the usefulness and efficiency of these weekly focus meetings? [remember, browbeating yourself does no good. You want your troubleshooting to be about inspiring yourself not flogging].

How is your use of an online calendar going to block off your time for various tasks? Are you able to batch similar types of tasks together? Are you getting lost in the weeds of the details, losing track of your big priorities? Wildly misestimating how much time you need for research, trouble-shooting, brainstorming? Do you charge hard for days then burn out?

What is your tendency with your calendar? What's one or two small steps of change you can make? Dial it back to food, mental health, exercise, or another of the earlier lessons if that is what's needed to properly troubleshoot your learning curve and keeping it flowing. As you work through this book, you should be naturally growing more skillful in wielding your time to maximum effect. Take some time today and this weekend to mull over where and how your time is getting blocked up. Try to frame your process as an exciting opportunity to lift yourself up, rather than seeing it as a dead weight that you're trying to unload.

WEEK 4
INTERNET PLATFORMS

Monday: Why It Matters

Integrating internet platforms into your workflow can save you a lot of time, as well as make your business more professional and customer-service oriented.

This week, I cover a few different programs' features. Remember, too much change is as destabilizing as too little change. Don't put off integrating these new programs, but be sure you don't get in over your head, and that every change gets stabilized into the daily and weekly processes of your business. It will most likely take a little trial and error to find the best fits, and to find the sweet spot of time invested to ROI.

This week, I'll present a lot of information and options, and Friday we'll build the plan for integrating. Remember, these are things you can return to later. It's all about you managing your time to best effect, not trying to make me happy. I present what I learned and did to succeed, you optimize my insights for your best effect.

Tuesday: Google

Google has quite a few features that make running a business a lot easier to manage.

Google Voice gives you a free phone number that you can associate with your business. You can set up hours for it to be available and you can send free texts. You can set a number up for your business, and you can also set up a number for yourself, that way you can separate work and personal without having 2 phones.

Google Drive, Docs, and Sheets allow you to easily share information with staff. Using Google Drive for all your business documents is an excellent way to stay organized and maintain version control on various documents. It is also an excellent tool for training staff, organizing and preparing for staff meetings, and giving your staff opportunities to demonstrate enthusiasm and leadership.

Google Calendar is an excellent way to stay organized and help you and your staff communicate about time. You can set up multiple calendars, so you can have a calendar for vacations and schedules, one for marketing campaigns, and one for weekly/monthly tasks. You can set it up to receive a daily email of your key tasks/events for the day as well. Having a software calendar makes scheduling and managing your time much easier.

Other programs exist that offer all these features. Google is great because it is free (or if you are a nonprofit, you might be able to receive more features for free or a reduced rate), and because it is an integrated system, versus having various different software for each of those features.

Take a few minutes to research further into these features. Take some notes on the pros and cons. What do you need to consider in order to incorporate software with these features into your business?

Wednesday: Twitter

There are over 300 million people on Twitter. It is an excellent, low-cost method of connecting with customers. Twitter can help you increase brand awareness, provide customer support, and connect with customers to develop trust, authenticity, and insight into their needs.

You can do market research into the conversations your target audience is having in order to better understand and connect with their pain points.

You can have real-time dialogue with both angry and happy customers in order to build strong relationships.

You can run promotions, conduct opinion polls, push educational content, as well as join groups to share info and increase brand awareness.

If you are feeling overwhelmed at getting into the world of Twitter, is there someone on your staff who would be interested in this growth opportunity?

The other option is, to start slow. Commit to spending 10 minutes two times a week either researching Twitter, or experimenting with using it. It might help with the overwhelm to initially focus only on developing your Twitter account for market research, running campaigns/increasing dialogue, or customer support.

Even if you're not quite ready for Twitter, start researching and learning about it. Even if you scoff at it, and never use it, as an open-minded small business owner, you should be aware of the tool and its utility and reach.

Thursday: ScheduleOnce and Hootsuite

A lot of time can get easily eaten up in booking and managing appointments. One of the easiest ways to save yourself time and make your customers happier is a software for scheduling.

ScheduleOnce integrates with both Google and Zapier. So, your client goes to your website, sees what times are available, books the appointment. They get a notification that they are booked, then they get a notification that their appointment is right around the corner. Your calendar automatically populates with the booking. All you had to do was set the program up, and it takes care of everything else for you.

There are other options available. I prefer this one because of how it integrates with Google and Zapier. As you get more sophisticated and up to speed with all the various software options, integration across programs is something you are going to need to become more mindful of.

Hootsuite is an excellent tool for staying up to speed across multiple social media accounts. You can use Hootsuite as your central site for running campaigns across multiple social media platforms like Facebook, Twitter, and Instagram. It also has a lot of other great features like planning your posts in advance, having an approval authority so you can delegate writing posts to staff, but still review them before they go live, and more.

Friday: Your Plan for Platform Integrations

We've covered a lot of different programs. Take a moment to think about where your biggest workflow impediment is---or if your biggest problem is customer churn, not enough eyeballs, not hitting revenue goals, or something else.

Which of the programs listed above can best help you meet that need? Focus there. Create your timeline for learning the program, incorporating, troubleshooting, and automating usage.

MONTH EIGHT
TIME & FINANCES MANAGEMENT

We all understand that time and money are two of our most precious resources when it comes to running and growing a business.

But we don't always know how to make adjustments to how we manage those resources, and our bad habits and lack of clear thinking around our time and money can be a major impediment to truly accelerating your business. As the saying goes, you get out what you put in, so it's time to learn to be smarter with how you put your time and money into your business.

Once I implemented all of these techniques, I had the time, knowledge, and financial resources to expand. I was able to invest in other projects such as real estate, as well as create other small businesses. I got to help design and launch a video game! I still am involved in the day-to-day of my business, but I get to invest myself in other fun projects I never would have had the opportunity for if I hadn't automated my business.

We've covered delegation. We've covered scheduling research and having the right approach to planning changes and improvements to health, marketing, software, staff, and the appearance of your storefront. We've talked about the importance and power of self-reflection and being honest. The other chapters of this book help you determine what to invest your time and money in. This chapter helps you improve how you go about investing on a day to day level.

WEEK 1
DISTRACTION AND FOCUS

Monday: Why It Matters

The science is in. It is possible to train your brain to consistently achieve high levels of focus.

You know those times when you are crushing it? Those times where you can feel the clarity of your mind radiating out through every word, every decision? Those times where your mind is awash in new insights? Those times where you get so focused and involved in what you're doing so that hours disappear without you realizing it?

How frequent are those for you? Do you feel that its more often the case that your mind is cluttered and busy, that you get pulled into tasks that don't really matter or aren't even connected to your business? Do you feel that you have tons of great ideas for improving and expanding your business, but never quite manage to implement them? Or are you more the type that struggles to come up with ideas you think are worth anything?

Well, with the material this week, you are going to learn how to more consistently achieve what many call "high states of flow," where your mind is sharp and you accomplish more in 15 minutes than it used to take in an hour.

Take a moment to examine these two states of mind in the past week in your life.

What time of day do you feel your mind is at its sharpest and most creative? In the morning? Afternoon? Evening? After working out?

After taking a break in nature? Search your memories for those times in the past week when your mind was on-point and write some observations about what you think contributed to that level of focus.

Now, do the same for the opposite state of mind. Search your memories for moments where your mind was dull and sluggish. Where you spent hours surfing websites when you meant to be working. Where your thoughts were moving too fast and disjointedly for you to be really successful at the task at hand. What happened in the 2-24 hours prior that might have contributed to that state of mind?

Tuesday: Adding Habits That Help You Focus

Behavior science in the past 10 years has uncovered quite a bit about how to achieve higher levels of focus.

For me, it all starts with being healthy. When I take care of my body, I take care of my mind. My best habit for keeping my mind focused and alert is exercise in the morning and evening. Exercise gets my blood flowing and oxygenated, and podcasts inspire me, give me new insights and tricks to try, and get me psyched up to take on the challenges of the day.

That's what works for me. For you it might be classical music in the car or at your desk. It might be starting every workday with tidying your office space. Whatever it is, consistency and diligence. Don't do it half-hearted part of the time. Don't do it to feed doubt or self-recrimination. The art is learning to do to feed your focus in a way that fits with you as a unique human being.

Science of Habit Change

I share this to help you effectively implement this information, vastly improving your focus, which will improve how you use and invest your time, which will reap dividends for your business.

Step 1. The first step is observation of what's really going on. Having an intellectual understanding of why something is good for you, or just using willpower to make yourself change doesn't work. What works is noticing, "hey, that big plate of pasta and bread I eat with my friend every Monday makes me feel really tired and dull all afternoon." Really feeling your reaction to that observation is what motivates you to change.

We all know this in some way: we've all been hit over the head with the sinking realization that we made a huge mistake that then motivated us to change our behavior so we never made that mistake again. We can deliberately use that process on the small stuff that doesn't hurt very much in the moment but with repetition ends up hurting a lot, like poor diet or sleep, or having our Facebook browser open while trying to work. With the small stuff that adds up over time, it takes a little initial effort to get used to really feeling the implications of our choices, but once you've practiced it, it becomes second nature.

Step 2. The second step, after having deliberate internal observation of the consequences of our choices, is adding small habits that move us in the right direction. Cutting out bad habits is only so effective without having good habits there to take their place. If eating a candy bar every afternoon provides emotional comfort and a sense of relaxation, then just cutting the treat out isn't going to get you very far, because you still need that afternoon moment of sweet relaxation, and your will power is probably only going to be able to hold out so long before caving to that very real need.

So the art and science of observation takes some trial and error. It takes some effort to uncover the motivators for those bad habits that wreck your focus, and figure out habits that get you that same great effect without the negative ones that come along with your current fix.

Look over your observations about what behaviors contributed to a sluggish or unfocused mind last week. Maybe you've thought of a few more to add to the list. What very real need do you see those habits feeding? I'm guessing a lot of it is stress reduction. Which is why the book starts with diet and exercise. When we are stressed, depressed, anxious, or not in a calm state, we lose our ability to focus.

Observe, both in your mind and feel in your body, what behaviors that lead to a dull or unfocused mind do to help you alleviate stress. Take notes.

Having a full-body, sensory understanding is essential to making adjustments to how you get into a state of focus. The list of focus enhancers that we cover tomorrow will only get you so far if you are just using willpower to make them stick.

Wednesday: Habits to Enhance Focus

There are a ton of daily practices you can do to increase your ability to focus and think clearly throughout the day. I will give you a list, but the biggest value-added of this week is my emphasis on sensory awareness and slow and steady change. Like I said yesterday, and the day before, you have to take the time to be aware of the subtle effects of your small daily habits that either help or hinder your focus.

Diet & Exercise. The biggest and most obvious focus- enhancing changes are here. Maybe go back and review that month to see how else you can improve your routines.

If you work out in the evening as part of unwinding for the day, you might consider either switching your routine to the morning or afternoon, or adding some small fitness activities during one or both of those times. Exercise oxygenates the brain and gets the nervous system aligned. Starting your day with a brain and nervous system functioning well sets the tone for the whole day. Also, from sitting long periods the body's systems start to get sluggish. Adding a little physical activity at least once during the workday can have a noticeable effect on focus.

Consider adding to your physical practices like martial arts, yoga, or tai chi, as these are all designed to be physically invigorating in a way that enhances the mind's ability to focus. 10-15 minutes in the morning or after lunch of a physical practice that is designed to enhance your ability to focus will have exponential effects on your ability to focus.

A set routine for your morning and evening wind-down. Automation isn't just good for your website's ability to generate leads. Automation can also help you focus and use your time more efficiently.

The beginning of your day sets the tone. If you roll out of bed and start reading emails in a haphazard and sporadic fashion, you are encouraging that energy to occur the rest of the day. I know it is easy to think that we need to get out of bed and hop right into activity, but in reality, it is the judicious use of rest and pauses and stillness that make activity efficient and productive. Not only with a good night's sleep, but also with how you start your day.

Ideally, you will have a firm habit of setting aside electronics for the first hour of your day. Spend that hour not only getting ready, but also connecting with your body and with the physical reality around you. Simply sitting with a cup of coffee by a window and observing the weather and whatever happens to be in the view of your window might not seem like it can increase your productivity and focus, but in the long run, it reaps huge benefits. The mind needs time to just be, to warm up, before you fill it with activity and complex thinking.

And automating this tranquility into your morning routine will help you build momentum towards making all the other changes you want or need to make to accelerate your business.

Remembering to be playful. Curiosity is a powerful, positive force. It increases our ability to absorb information. It often leads us down paths that have benefits we never could have imagined. It is the inspiration and motivation for positive change. Curiosity requires a sense of playfulness. If we are burdened by stress, we are undermining our capacity for curiosity. Taking the time to be truly playful and lighthearted can have tremendous impacts on your ability to focus.

But, curiosity can't be forced. You can't dictate playfulness. Think about things or moments where you have felt playful. What inspired them, or helped create them?

Most of these ideas only take a few minutes a day. If you've been exercising regularly and eating healthier, you already know the power that small daily changes can have on your life. Create a plan for implementing some small changes in your habits.

Thursday: Habits to Subtract

Once you've made steps to add focus-enhancing habits, it is easier to start to cut out those habits that get in your way.

The biggest detriments to focus that I have seen are:

Multitasking. We all know that multitasking is counterproductive. And yet we all think we are the exception. The simple truth is, when you multi-task, you corrupt your ability to focus. Examine the past few work days and look for habits of when you try to do two (or more!) things at once. Make a plan for quitting this bad habit and you will reap huge rewards in productivity.

Multi-tasking has its place. I drive and listen to podcasts, for instance. But overburdening your mind by trying to cram cram cram, do do do, is only going to lead to burn-out. So look at where you are trying to shove too much into too little of time, and come up with a plan for change.

Disorganized email inboxes. Just like how our minds can't truly focus if we are trying to do multiple things at once, our minds can't focus if there are too many 'to-do's' on the backburner, and email inboxes are a seemingly infinite source of to-do's. Subconsciously, every time we open our email and have a long list of emails in there, our mind adds opening and reading them all to the to-do list. It might not seem like much, but it is a real strain on the mind that subtly leads to and feeds disorganization and chaos.

Starting and ending every day with an empty email inbox is great for your mind, and has all kinds of other benefits in terms of time-management efficiency.

First, unsubscribe or block every email list that doesn't match your priorities. Create rules so that emails that matter don't go directly to your inbox, but rather to folders such as 'to-do' 'personal correspondence' 'marketing research,' etc.

If you have the emails you want go directly to certain folders, then the random flow of emails into your inbox will not distract and dictate your time. You can then block out times to go into certain folders and knock out the emails in that folder, rather than a hodgepodge of dealing with emails.

The phone and internet. Phones and the internet are designed to suck us in, using a sophisticated understanding of how the human attention span works. Having your phone volume on, or an internet browser open, is basically multitasking and has that same disruption of focus. You can use an app to block the internet. You can turn your phone off, or on silent or priority call when you need to focus.

It is best to create a routine, so you can train your mind to be ready to focus. Pick the time slots where you need to have the highest level of focus and attention to the task at hand, and create a viable plan for cutting these things from being able to disrupt you.

Not having, or sticking to, a plan. When you set an intention and then don't follow through, you are undermining your ability to focus. That's why I recommend starting your day with your top 3 priorities, and having agenda-setting meetings once a week. Of course, it takes time to get good at estimating your ability to accomplish what you set out to do, with the time and resources you have, but getting consistent with starting your day with your daily tasks, and starting your week with your vision for the week helps you focus and learn to be a true master of managing your time.

Friday: Implementation

We have covered a ton of information this week. You are most likely not going to be able to implement everything at once.

Take some time to think about what your biggest detriment to focus is and create a plan for automating better habits.

Also, block off 30 minutes on your calendar a month from now with the task to review how your progress is, and add another 1-2 of these habits of focus to your routine.

WEEK 2
"HOT COOKIE THEORY"

Monday: Why It Matters

When the cookie is hot--when the leads come in, when they really want your service--what do you do?

A lady I know runs a massage business. Sara has a website and business cards, and relies mostly on word-of-mouth. She has a steady clientele of loyal regulars, but she secretly hopes to have 5 more customers. She's afraid to admit this out loud, except with her sister. She also teaches a yoga class at the studio where she hosts massage workshops during the summer.

Where is the hot cookie? On the surface, it might not look like there are any. But actually there are at least 3 hot cookies that she is letting slide by. Partly for psychological reasons (i.e., lack of self-confidence, fear of the unknown), but also partly from just not knowing where the opportunity is.

First hot cookie is the incredible loyalty of her regulars. Waiting around for them to recommend her might be 'working,' but it doesn't lead to business acceleration. She needs to be experimenting with ways to inspire and motivate them to more consistently spread the word about her skills.

Second hot cookie is the yoga studio she has a connection with. Those workshops and yoga classes are prime opportunities for encouraging and motivating people to take the next step of scheduling a massage. Workshops are a great way for her to expand her business model and think about shifting from solely working 1-1 to other creative ways to expand her reach and customer base.

The third she isn't capitalizing on is that website. We dive into that tomorrow. Today, take a moment to make a big picture assessment of your business, and think about the spaces where either ignorance of techniques/tools or psychological blockers are holding you back from enjoying that hot cookie.

Tuesday: Auto-email Campaigns

Email campaigns are one of the most efficient ways you can be ready for when the cookie is hot out of the oven. If someone goes to your website, or sends you an email, you should have an automatic email campaign that begins when they first reach out.

Now, remember, it is critical that your email campaign is authentic, adds value, and builds trust.

Take a few moments and describe the demographics of 2 groups of people (3 if you have other ways for people to become part of emails, such as via staff encouragement when they are in your physical store space).

What do you know about the people who click to your website?

What do you know about the people sending you an email?

What are their motivations? Are they curious? Do they have a spark or do they need you to spark them? What is their pain point? What information do they need in order to become convinced to exchange value with you?

Mull this over. Do some data analytics, talk it over with staff. You need to get really clear about who these leads are before you draft your email campaign.

Sara thought about her clientele. She realized that most of them are retirees, semi-retired, or close to retirement. Most of them are female, and have a close group of friends and family that live in town. She generated these ideas for bringing in new leads:

o Galentine's partner massage workshop
o discount for scheduling before/after a vacation
o keep thinking of other potential ways to encourage regulars to recommend to friends, deals on gift cards during holidays, etc
o see if she can listen more deeply to conversations to better understand the pain points in her clientele's social circles, to use to generate different ideas for workshops
o potential discounts for encouraging her massage clients to attend her yoga classes

All of these ideas have the potential to generate more ideas for email campaign content and strategies for when and how to launch.

Sara decides to put all these ideas on the backburner, using her calendar and weekly planning sessions to block out the time across the next 6 months. She decides that the most important priority for right now is to encourage everyone she knows to sign up to her mailer.

…which for her means deciding how to have a mailer. She realizes she needs to set up an email campaign for people who attend her workshops in the summer. She wants to keep it simple. She decides to set up 2 campaigns. One that lets people who've attended know about upcoming workshops, and one around Thanksgiving (her slowest season) to encourage workshop attendees to try a massage during the stressful holiday season.

Your turn. Maybe you don't get to the point where you know what kinds of campaigns you run today, but at least begin with pinpointing your audience and getting a sense of where the easiest, best priority lies.

Wednesday: Draft your Auto-email Campaign

Now that you've got a sense of who you are connecting with through your email campaign, it is time to draft it. –And if you're not at drafting, keep brainstorming ideas for what you want that campaign to be, and adjust your personal timeline for this project accordingly. If that's not a skill you've developed yet, return to chapter and work through that material again. Treat this book like you are building muscle strength over time, not like you *should* be some kind of superhero who gets it all right yesterday.

What is the measurable goal of this campaign? What specific action do you want them to take at the end?

Sara has 2 measurable goals. She wants to convert 20% of workshop attendees into repeat customers. She also wants to convert 20% of workshop attendees to massage clients.

Remember—Sara only wants to gain 5 new customers. Her goals for accelerating her business are not your goals. My goals for my businesses are not your goals. What we all have in common is a desire for growth, and an interest in taking care of automating how we recognize and enjoy that hot cookie that looks delicious and just right for our business model and goals.

Use the following questions to help you generate ideas.

What can you do to demonstrate your value? Can you provide a special offer? What are their doubts going to be, and how can you head those off at the pass?

Do you need to delegate the email campaign? Do you need to do more research on good email campaigns? Do you need your mentor to look over your campaign before you launch it?

How are you going to measure the results of your campaign, so that next time you will be able to learn from this one and do an even better job?

Look to month 9 in this book for more insight into your campaign if you feel ready. Otherwise, go ahead and treat this as a trial run on the more in-depth and iterative process of funnels that we will get to soon.

Remember, you want to have a clear call to action for your leads. Remember that you are building trust. Remember that you need to stay on-brand with your promises.

Thursday: Automate, the Cookie is Hot

How else do leads come in, and how else can you automate being ready while the cookie is hot?

Remember how Sara thought of multiple ideas, but put most of them either on the backburner, or kept in the 'gather more data' phase? You don't have to do it all right now. Today I want you to keep brainstorming, and get organized on where you store those ideas to use at a pre-determined future date. Take advantage of those calendar functions and software programs.

The following questions can help you generate creative ideas that fit with *your* goals. Remember, Sara took her goal of 5 new massage clients, converted that into income, realized she could hit that income goal with her workshops if she did a better job inspiring repeat customers, and also did a better job getting their emails and using that to offer deals and encourage workshop attendees to convert to massage clients.

If you have people coming to your physical storefront, how can you train your staff to build loyalty with the leads?

If you have a group of customers, how can you offer them new, or added value, so that they are further committed to your brand? (i.e., if you have a local gym, can you sell t-shirts?).

If you struggle to get people scheduled, can you automate your calendar?

Brainstorm other ideas. First, you have to identify where you can become more efficient, like how Sara realized how inefficient she was with her workshops and gathering emails and setting up automated campaigns. Then, you can start to tap your inner creative visionary.

Test your ideas--get input. Then, create your plan for improving how you build trust and authenticity with your leads, so that you can improve your conversion rate.

Friday: Automate Your Automation Processes

Sara decided to set aside 3 hours on the last Friday of every month to look over her email campaigns, brainstorm, and decide what needed to be implemented or done in the month ahead for her to continue to move toward her goals for growth.

That way, she knew when she needed to think about it, and could set it aside to take care of the day-to-day. She started keeping a notebook to jot ideas down in, and at the end of every day, she'd transfer the notes to whatever file, Google event, or task, needed to be the storage spot for that idea.

Jotting down and transferring little notes takes Sara all of a few minutes each day. It does wonders for her ability to focus.

With that sort of automation for generating ways to enjoy that hot cookie, she's taken a weight of stress and doubt off her mind, sleeps better at night, and her regulars have been commenting on a new level of cheerful energy they've noticed.

Maybe you schedule weekly time. Where my business is at, I have 3-5 meetings a week with various staff groups. We do small check-ins on campaigns on an almost daily basis. I sit down with myself once a week to look at the big picture and look over all the ideas and goals that are bubbling on the stove, that I'd like to get cooking on in the near future. Be prepared to experiment to find your sweet spot. Take some time right now to look at your goals, your learning curve, your specific targets and your current state of your plans for meeting them. Then pull out your calendar and see what needs to happen.

Automation takes trial-and-error, consistent effort, and an open mind. If you need to go back to previous material, don't let your ego ignore the simple reality of what you need so that you can get where you want to go. I still take classes and listen to podcasts on emails and social media, and I know enough to write a book on it! What I listen to has changed, but I am still always learning and experimenting and trying new things.

WEEK 3
BE THE VISIONARY, NOT THE IMPLEMENTER

Monday: Why It Matters

We think we can do it all. We are ambitious—that's what gave us the ability to start and run a small business. That ambition and drive is crucial to entrepreneurial success. But, I have seen time and again how people micromanage, try to do it all, avoid learning and trying new things, and get lost in the weeds and then their vision does not truly become implemented.

Your job is to see the vision. I like to use the metaphor of chess. You aren't one side or the other, you aren't implementing the moves for either side. You are the one with the vision of the game overall, that allows both sides to play, learn, and accomplish whatever their goals are for entering the game. It is your job to observe how the game plays out, so that you can make adjustments so that both your customers and your staff increase the values that they have set out to increase.

Take a moment to reflect on your skills, beliefs, and habits around how you choose to divide your time with your business. How hard was it for you to get started with blocking off time for generating and implementing email campaigns? How successful are your weekly focus meetings? How stressed and busy do you feel?

Reflect a little on where things are. Be real with yourself, but don't go into analytical overdrive.

Tuesday: Invest in your Staff's Ability to Implement

We have talked about this in the month on taking care of your staff, but everything connects when it comes to accelerating your business, so today we are circling back around to this concept of investing in your staff.

This might mean paying for some outside training, this might mean allocating some hours for them to self-learn, this might mean scheduling some time for observation and feedback, this might mean making some changes to your weekly meetings and training plan for the next quarter or year.

Investing in your staff's ability to implement your vision has 3 components:

o Refining current processes
o Getting ahead of the game when making changes to how your business operates
o Creating opportunities for your staff to bring their creativity and unique talents to the table

We talked earlier about using training and weekly meetings to refine current processes and to create opportunities for your staff to become leaders. Before moving on to getting ahead of the game, take a few moments to flip back to that chapter and assess whether or not you should invest some of your time into either of those two areas when it comes to improving your staff's ability to implement your vision.

Now let's talk about the skills as the visionary and delegator that you need for getting ahead of the game with your staff when it comes to making changes to your business.

This is a challenging skill, and so I want you to be prepared to fail the first few times you practice this. But, if you invest in yourself to master this skill, you will be amazed at how much your business accelerates.

As we've been talking about throughout the book, as the visionary, you are imagining the future in such a way that you can return to the present and create a viable plan for bringing that vision of the future into fruition.

When you take this ability to the next level with your staff, you exponentially increase the capacity of your business to succeed.

We started to build this skill last week, with how we worked through generating automated email campaigns. Yesterday, we set this stage with reflecting on the status quo. Today, we add that next component of further developing the ability to realistically assess what's going on with staff.

Wednesday: Time to Revise your Quarter, Year, and 3-year Goals & Strategy

Let's get ambitious today. You've learned a lot these past 7.5 months. Everything you've learned needs to get integrated into your plan. Don't put it off.

What I want you to focus on is redesigning your plan so that you are focusing on more of your time being directed toward being the visionary, and not the implementer.

This has 2 components. One part is being more efficient with your own time, as we've been working toward throughout. The other is developing the ability to know what and when to hand off to others—and to ensure they are equipped for success. You own the business, you own the process.

One of the common mistakes I see is being unwilling to let go of doing tasks that are comfortable and known. A friend of mine used to be the manager of a department in his book-publishing organization. He sat on the board for reviewing manuscripts that came in. He read the final manuscripts before they were published. When he got promoted, he was unwilling to let go of those responsibilities and trust his staff to implement his vision. Plus, he just liked reading all the manuscripts, he felt good about himself when it came to that part of the company. He created a huge backlog, because he didn't really have the time to read every submitted manuscript, and read every final manuscript, because he had new responsibilities. But, it was his favorite part of the job, and maybe he didn't really trust his staff to get it right. Everything got jammed up. Books started being published late. Authors weren't hearing back if their manuscripts were accepted or rejected. If he had kept this up, he would have probably wrecked the reputation, and therefore the success, of the company, because authors would have gotten frustrated and left, and warned others to find somewhere else to publish their work.

It's human nature; it's perfectly normal to lose sight of the vision when big changes come along like that. It was his favorite part, and it was something that he was good at, but he forgot about the bigger vision and quit looking to the future he wanted to create.

Pull out your quarterly, yearly, and 3-year goals and strategies. Take some time to carefully think about where you really need to invest your time to reach those goals, where you are comfortable doing something but should let go of that responsibility to someone else. As a small business owner, it's not about staying comfortable, but being willing to learn new skills and take on new challenges so that your business can truly grow.

With all that in mind, find what goals or strategies need to shift so that more of your time can be as the visionary. We will be talking about this the rest of the week, so no need to get it all done, and all right today.

Thursday: Visionaries Oversee the Process

Like my friend I talked about yesterday, visionaries don't run the processes, they oversee the processes. Even if you have no employees, you want to adjust your mindset and your goals to acknowledge that hiring people—even just freelance, work-trade, or companies who sell you the goods you need to make your product—is part of business growth.

What processes, either at the day-to-day level, weekly, or monthly level, are you spending too much of your time in, that could be better handed to someone else? Create a plan and incorporate into your overall strategy for handing that off and overseeing it, rather than running it. What do you need to do in order to have full trust in your staff or contracted worker for this to be a success?

The flip side is figuring out what to do with your freed up time once you've delegated implementation. We will talk about that tomorrow at the big-picture level. The rest of the chapters are also dedicated to where your time should go. Take some time today to catch up on all the work that I've been asking from you this month.

Friday: What You as the Visionary Are Responsible For

Understanding the market. This means having a clear understanding of what is going on with your target demographic, what problems you solve for them, and who else out there is solving that problem and how you stand out from them. This is taking care of the "hot cookie" like we talked about 2 weeks ago, and cover from other angles in other chapters.

Building rapport with staff, customers, and other business owners. You are the leader. Managing the skills and responsibilities of your staff; tuning in with your customers and making them feel like part of the family; observing what's going on in your neighborhood, town, city, market, state, etc are all essential components of communicating and refining the vision as your company moves through time.

Overseeing and improving processes. How the work gets done is up to your staff. Improving how the work gets done is up to your leadership. It's your job to know when to make changes to process, whether or not the idea for change comes from you, a staff member, or an article you read. This means continuing to learn new skills, new technologies, new ways to encourage your staff to be creative and driven.

Keeping an eye on 'the weather.' This includes technology trends, business trends, and shifts in your ecosystem (stuff that's happening in your city, or the spaces you occupy online). It also means keeping an eye on your internal state and personal life. Are you healthy? Happy? Achieving the goals and dreams that matter most to you in all aspects of life?

Setting measurable goals for growth of your business. Generally, measurable goals are increased revenue and more customers. But those measurable goals are influenced by all kinds of intangibles, such as trust, authenticity, brand awareness, and professionalism. It's your job to have a thorough understanding of the relationship between the intangibles and the measurable goals. For example, in a business where your staff offer their specialized skills (i.e., coaching, accounting, cooking, etc), the level of pride and inclusivity of that staff are integral to repeat customers.

Measurable goals tell you what is and isn't working. They give you direction and focus for generating new ideas, for learning new skills, and for enhancing the experience of customers and staff.

Deciding how your business is going to get more customers in the door, and make those customers feel the maximum amount of satisfaction with the value they received from their dollar being spent at your business. Of course, as a small business owner, you are going to have to be part of the work, you can't hand everything off to your staff. But, as I said Wednesday, you don't want to get lost in the weeds, just because you are comfortable doing the work there.

Look through the 6 things on this list. Look at how you spend your time on daily tasks, weekly tasks, monthly tasks. Look at your strategic plan. Where are things getting kinked up? What steps can you take? Where are your biggest priorities? Look at your calendar, your long-term goals, and work out how you are going to handle

o   Handing off tasks
o   Training and overseeing what you hand off
o   Generating new marketing strategies

o   Keeping up-to-date on all details and data

We're in Month 8. You've already developed all the skills I am asking you to implement today. We are just taking it to the next level. Remember, if you need to go back to an earlier chapter to refine a certain skill, don't sell yourself short by ignoring the truth. But—don't sell yourself short by avoiding that next big leap into unfamiliar terrain.

WEEK 4
USING THE MONEY YOU MAKE TO MAKE YOU MORE MONEY

Monday: Why It Matters

Money can often create emotional and psychological knots in our system that we don't even recognize. We all learned beliefs about how money works when we were kids that we play out as adults. It is crucial—if you want to accelerate your business—that you improve your ability to make rational decisions about money that truly help you achieve your vision.

We cover this topic as part of time/focus, because investing in thinking rationally about how you spend your time and cultivate or disrupt your ability to focus helps to lay the groundwork for thinking more rationally about what you do with your money as a small business owner.

Using the money you make to make you more money is a big topic. We will cover some business-accelerating tips on how to better care for the money flow from a range of angles.

Tuesday: Be Willing to Pay People For Things That Aren't A Valuable Use of Your Time

I see people thinking irrationally about this all the time. Your time is incredibly valuable. Your skills as a business owner are skills nobody else in your business has. Therefore, your time should be dedicated to those things, and other people should take care of the other stuff.

Let's say your time is valued at $50 an hour. And every year you spend about 10 hours putting together your taxes. That's $500 dollars worth of time that you could have better invested elsewhere-like say creating a dynamite marketing plan that brought you 10 new loyal customers. You could have spent $300 on an accountant—who would save you more money with their insight into tax deducations—and not only saved the $200, but gained from what you did choose to invest all the time into.

So, even if it only takes you 5 hours to do your taxes, you are still making more money overall by paying someone else to do what they are good at and use your time for investing in part of your business that only you can do. That 5 hours put into a marketing campaign that brought you 10 new regular, loyal customers makes way more sense than taking on doing your taxes with that time!

This principle can be applied to all areas of your life. If you've been doing web design because you are trying to be frugal, have you really stepped back and determined whether or not it is worth your valuable time, or if you'd be better off paying someone else to do it, and putting your time into something only you can do?

Take a few minutes to brainstorm some areas where it might be worth it for you to pay someone else. Map out how much time it would save, what you would invest that time in, and how you are going to go about finding the right person to pay to take that task off your hands.

Wednesday: Invest in your Education

Of course, it isn't a clear 1-1 where you pay more money for education and you get more out of it. Life isn't that simple. But as a business owner in a constantly changing market, you need to recognize that regular investment in your education (and the education of your employees) is necessary for the long-term growth and stability of your business.

You don't want to invest in learning skills or concepts that overall don't make the best use of your time. For example, it would be a bit of a waste to take some classes on filing your tax returns when you could be taking classes on the latest marketing tactics. Investing your time and money into your education should be done with care and a clear sense of how it connects to your long-term vision and goals.

I do recommend that every business owner invest in their diet and exercise. As we talked about in Chapter 1 (A Healthy You = A Healthy Business). It is worth it to pay for a trainer and/or nutritionist. You get more done, and do it better, when you are healthy. Besides, what's the point of having a successful business if you are too sick, exhausted, or weak to really enjoy it?

There is a lot of brilliant research and thinkers in the business world today. There are a lot of areas available to you to invest in your learning.

Before you decide what your education priorities are, look over your long-term goals. How are you planning to grow your company in the next 3 years? That will help you determine where to invest in learning.

Something else I tell everyone is to invest in attending conferences. I also tell everyone to invest in a mentor with the skills and ability to help you see the truth about what is, and what is not working with your business. We all have blind spots, and skilled mentors who can coach you through improvement are worth the investment.

For example, say for your business you spend a lot of time talking with clients. It might be worth your time to invest in a voice coach. Or maybe it would be worth it to invest in having a voice coach train your staff. Investing in education doesn't always necessarily mean business coaches. If you want to develop your ability to think creatively so you can come up with better marketing campaigns, you might hire a meditation coach, build a relationship with a therapist so you can unblock your psyche, or learn how to doodle. Or something else entirely might be the right investment for you to develop your creativity.

The other thing I always tell small business owners is to invest in the strengths you already have. The ones that are the heart of the success of your business.

There are 3 areas of investment: knowledge, skills, and relationships. Investment in education is a combination of investing your time and your money. So, now it's time to step back and look at the big picture before coming up with a plan to invest in your education.

First, look at your long-term goals. Then, look at your finances and time. Then, think about whether you need more knowledge, improved skills, or improved (or more) relationships.

Take some time now to consider the material from today, and begin to get a sense of where you need to invest your time. Give yourself about a week to mull it over. Perhaps create a reminder so you think about this for a few minutes every day. Block out time after your week of consideration to develop your step-by- step plan for investing in your education (and perhaps your staff as well) across the next year.

Take notes in your notebook.

Thursday: Invest Outside your Business

Not only do you need to be putting money into your business, in the form of education, staff, capital, but you also need to create some stability and security for yourself by investing your earnings outside your business.

You need to do your due diligence and research, network, and ask hard questions to the point where you land yourself a great financial advisor. If you are going to invest in stocks, learn enough to ask good questions of your potential advisor; if you are going to invest in land or rental property, do your research; if you are going to invest in bonds, do your research.

If all your capital is tied up in your business, this might need to be your priority for investing in your own education for the year ahead.

Many small business owners do not think ahead to their retirement. The common wisdom states you want to be saving at least 20% of your yearly income for retirement. Yes, you can rely on your business for some of that, but build some safety in and find some areas outside your business to grow your money in.

I want to emphasize—yes, again—the importance of doing your research, and doing your due diligence toward picking the right area to invest your money in, and the right person to help guide you in that investment. Tap your network for insight and potential leads on amazing financial advisors.

Create your plan in the space below for beginning to gather information towards successful investment outside your business.

First, what questions do you have that you will need answers to?

Second, who do you know that you can ask these questions of? (and you will want to ask the same question of multiple people)

Third, where do you think it makes the most sense for you to invest? Rental, stocks, bonds, retirement funds, or a mix? If you don't know, that means you have some more questions to add to the space above.

Fourth, what misgivings, concerns, worries, etc, do you have about beginning this process? Does it seem overwhelming? Like a bad idea? Like it's not worth it? Take a few minutes to breath slowly and deeply, really feeling where in your body you experience the resistance to this step. Write down your insights in your journal.

Friday: You're Going to Make Mistakes

Like I said Monday, there's often a lot of psychological backlog when it comes to money. You cannot let being afraid of making mistakes continue to be a hang-up.

Learn from one of my mistakes: Don't invest in a business idea where the other person doesn't have skin in the game. 6 years ago I invested money with someone to open up a business.

But the person I was investing with wasn't financially involved. He had the necessary skills to run the business. But he didn't invest financially. At the time, I didn't think anything of it.

80% of the way into opening the business, the person I was partnering up with said, "You know what, I changed my mind I don't want to do this anymore." 80% of the way in meant that I had already invested in all of the supplies, etc that we needed to open. I was already 100% committed. Because he didn't have anything to lose, it was easy for him to back out. As he backed out he left me in a hole.

I learned from my mistake, I didn't just give up on partnering with others to open new businesses. I'm working with someone right now where we opened a new business together—this time though, I made sure we both had skin in the game.

Mistakes are going to happen. It's all about what you do with them that defines whether or not your long-term trajectory is one of growth and acceleration or not.

MONTH NINE
CLOSING THE SALE

With the rapid rise of technology, closing the sale often feels like it is not as simple as it used to be. I know when I had all those competitors opening up near me, I got worried. But I developed new skills and practices and my business continues to grow. Once you have mastered the basics of these new ways of engaging with leads, building trust and interest, persuading people of your value, and encouraging them to return, you will be a master of automation, and it will feel simple to you.

But, it takes sweat and patience to get there, just like it takes sweat and patience to improve your health. This month, we begin with an overview of the 'soft skills' of closing the sale. Developing the soft skills is essential to creating email campaigns, and email campaigns are an essential part of closing the sale. In this age of information overwhelm, part of your job as a business owner is to keep a beacon lit so that those who could benefit from what you offer have the easiest pathway possible to understanding your brand, and creating the feeling that they are getting a great value for their dollar time and again. As Gary Vanerchuk says, we have to keep building know, like, and trust. Without that emphasis and art, the technical skills of software and ad campaigns can only go so far.

After we cover the soft skills, in weeks 2 and 3 we go step-by-step through the process of developing an automated email campaign for you to begin using right away. I do recommend you wait to finalize and launch your campaign until you have read week 4, which returns to another 'soft skill' aspect of closing the sale: how to value your product, internally in your planning, and externally in your marketing.

WEEK 1
SELL WITH HONESTY

Monday: Why It Matters

As you well know, authenticity and trust are essential to the small business. Small businesses rely on repeat customers to grow, because people return to spend somewhere they had a great experience. It's not true just for the entertainment industry. And small businesses get repeat customers when they have a great product, and are authentic and trustworthy.

It's a craft, an art form. In my industry, I focus on taking care of my staff, because that care translates over into how they interact with the customers. The respectful, honest relationships we cultivate cross over into their rapport-building with clients. I also have regular training and conversations where we talk honestly about the skills of rapport-building.

So, there is nothing I can do or say, really, that is going to wave some magic wand to make your product/service great—that is on you! But when you take care of your body, when you self-reflect often, and are always striving to learn, then you can trust that the quality of your goods and services is excellent. We all know that old story about the tree in the woods—if you aren't standing tall, speaking firmly and passionately about the excellence of what you are selling, then not much is going to happen. So, learning those soft skills of communication is essential to success.

Take a moment to reflect on your inner sense of self-worth and its connection to your inner sense of the worth and value of your company. It's easy to get those tangled up, and it's easy to project your personal self-doubt or life stress onto your business. We've all done it. The weekly focus meeting, the eating and exercising, the development of an open, learner's mindset all work together to get you over that hump. This week, we'll work on the soft skills. Today, I just want you to open your mind to old memories, to who you used to be, to who you want to be, and what skills or inner changes rise up from that reflection that help you understand how to open up to taking that next step.

Tuesday: Understand Their Business, Their Needs, Their Pain Points

In order to close the sale, you must have a genuine and thorough understanding of the slice of humanity that is the pool of potential purchasers of your product or service. We cover this in more detail next month, if you want to skip ahead to do that work before continuing here. However, I have confidence that you know enough about who is interested in your service to go ahead and launch a successful automated email campaign.

Humans still have that edge over machines in terms of refined ability to apply discretion and intuitive judgment to complexities, particularly when it comes to why people do what they do.

And you need to thoroughly understand why people do what they do in order to close the sale, both in person, and in the creation of automated campaigns that we will be setting up this month.

So, look over your notes on what people have said about why they go to you, talk with your employees, your network, look over your competition or your notes on your competition. Take today to immerse yourself in exploring and thinking about what is going on in the reality of people—those who purchase from you already, and that group that you just know would benefit immensely from what you have to offer.

There are 3 main facets to this process, that are iterative in nature. You want to have a gauge on how, why, when, and where people decide to spend money at your store. Your CRM, your social media presence, and your other forms of feedback from customers gives you some of this information.

You want to know, in detail, who your ideal customer is. You want to know typical demographics, the statistics, but without losing that human element of hopes and dreams, fears, pain, problems and goals (covered next month if you want to flip ahead for some insight).

You also want to know about your competition. Who else does what you do, nearby, online, at the national or regional level? What other businesses compete with your business? How do they position themselves, how do you stand out?

Start letting these questions percolate in your brain. Jot down notes, make observations, spark your creativity. We'll put this information to use next week. Starting this immersion will set you up for better success once you start designing that next marketing campaign this month.

Wednesday: Your Discomfort Impedes the Sales Process

Take advantage of silence. Silence is an art, not a bullet list of behaviors to perform. It requires a tuning in to the moment that being healthy supports. That's why we started with your health, because it is your health combined with your passion and attention to detail that are the heart and soul of your business.

Maintain a sincere and simple belief in the quality of your goods/ services. Any negative thoughts that you have about your business should be examined for validity, and then dispelled. It is human nature to take a kind of comfort from certain topics of negative habits of thinking, and you need to tame it, or it is going to get in your way.

Don't gloss over the price. If you are uncomfortable about the price, you are going to implicitly convey that to your potential new client. The whole point of a sale is to trade money for goods or a service, by sidestepping a frank conversation about price, you are getting in your own way. It is important to have a discussion of pricing as part of your roadmap. A clear and simple explanation of what a customer is paying for helps build trust and encourage them to spend their money with you.

Pull out your roadmap for engaging with leads. Where is the conversation about price? Is it a straightforward part of your process? Do you address customer thoughts or reservations about price? If not, add that now.

Also, take the time to look over your roadmap to revise for a better, simpler, clearer expression of your belief in the quality of your goods/services.

If you need, use your journal to brainstorm or write down some observations or notes.

Thursday: Personalize as much as Possible

As a small business, customers want to feel part of something unique. That comes from the authenticity of your brand, the clarity of your mission's effort to address the needs of customers, and from having a personalized experience that fits within brand and mission.

Personalized that fits within brand and mission requires you to be comfortable with your role as visionary, which hopefully you are at this point. If you're not, that is okay! Simply use your reservations as a guide to going back to previous chapters to study and utilize to make changes.

Take some time today, or block out time during the next week to research how your competition personalizes. Research related industries as well. Take brief notes as you research, and block out time a few days later to look over your notes. Having a few days between note-taking and reviewing gives time for your creativity to spark, which is where you are able to develop a unique idea or couple of ideas to create a more personalized experience that doesn't become a time or resource burden.

I like to go to conventions or conferences in an entirely different industry as inspiration. Immersing myself in another field fires up my zeal and gives my imagination all kinds of new thoughts to incorporate into my idea-generating. A lot of people like to spend quiet time in nature, that fuels up their inner creative. Maybe your creativity is fueled by an artistic pursuit you're 'bad' at, or by a martial art or other meditative discipline. Today, you are going to use research and observation to get those sparks of inspiration flying. Observing how other people achieve success is an excellent source of ideas.

Let your lead/customer talk. It is part of human nature to love to talk, to share our experience. Often, this is even more so when getting to share our perception of an experience to the person or persons who created it. In other words, it is human nature to love to share what our experience was with a business, service, or product. So much so that it's now its own industry, and an unquestioned and automatic part of the decision-making process with our purchasing power. We've already covered written reviews, which is a key aspect of 'letting clients talk.' Now we are going to cover the importance of letting your clients talk in person.

It's easy to dominate the conversation with your excitement, vision, and ideas about your business; to feel that sharing all that will get the potential customer as excited. But, what has demonstrated real results is creating space for people to share their thoughts and experiences and making your focus in the conversation to listen, connect, and learn.

This means developing the art and craft of the question, and the art and craft of 'say-back.'

Create a plan for developing your art of communication. Maybe you put it on the agenda for next quarter or next year. Maybe it's just taking time to reflect after talking with leads or observing how ads do online. Maybe you attend a training or hire a coach. You know your limits, experience, and goals. Incorporate some dedicated time for improvement into your schedule as it best meets your needs and demands.

Friday: Get to Clear Yeses or Nos, Not Maybes

With leads, it's better to have a clear no than a bunch of maybes. Maybes might pad your conversion rate numbers, but they can lead to you wasting your time and energy, and can compound confusion and ignorance around what is and isn't working. A 'no' doesn't mean forever, but it provides more information to help you improve than a maybe does.

Reflect on how you and your staff engage with customers. Are you too pushy to the point where people say maybe rather than no in order to escape the conversation? Or are you so gentle in your ask that everything feels like a maybe because you don't speak with enough clarity and conviction about their options?

If you are like most people, it's probably a mix and depends somewhat on the day. It takes being willing to have an honest and clear assessment of your actions to be able to refine this so that you are almost always seated comfortably in your own vision so that it translates well to others.

Block off time to either develop, or delegate to a staff member, or find someone to train you and relevant staff members to improve your soft skills. Remember from Month 1 on hiring a fitness trainer, if you are going to hire someone, be sure you have assessed their ability to competently train in this area. And also, make a thorough and unemotional assessment of whether or not it is worth it to invest in hiring someone to train you in this area. If you have the capital, you will get a huge return on investing in this area. But, we all know it's not always realistic, and such decisions are made from a centered awareness of the big picture of your particulars.

Staff training can be as simple as observing each other interact with leads and giving honest feedback. At this point in the book, you and your staff should have developed strong abilities to navigate honest feedback with one another. Be sure to be open to receiving feedback yourself. Your staff will be inspired by the simple act of acknowledging you are human.

WEEK 2
GETTING AUTOMATED FOR SPEED AND CONSISTENCY: WEBSITES, EMAILS, OPTING IN.

Monday: Why It Matters

The more you can add automation to your lead generation, lead conversion, and closing the sale, the better you are using your time. Your focus and goal for making changes to those 3 processes should be with an eye toward automation.

Automation increases the speed and reach of lead generation and sales. Automation also helps you increase the consistency of both.

This week we focus on automating the funnel from which leads happen upon your online presence and become inspired to participate in your online dialogue in the ways that you encourage through your automated processes.

For this week, 'closing the sale' means leads sign up for email campaigns or other automated content generation. When you are thinking about the long-term success of your business, the more you build a relationship with a lead, the more trust and authenticity exists in the relationship. You might not be used to thinking of an email campaign as a relationship, but they are.

Today, pick 5 companies to research. Use the parameters you think best for choosing those companies—ones that are in your field, bigger than you, the top of the industry, your direct competition, a company doing a similar thing in a different region, or pick one outside your field but whose brand or personality inspires you. Go to the websites, sign up for the email campaign. Use your notebook to make observations and compare and contrast.

Tuesday: The Overview of Email Campaigns: What They Are, Why They Matter

The world is very full, and very busy. Everyone has a lot going on. Email campaigns are an ideal way to remind them of their interest in your business, and to encourage them to fully see the genuine value of what you have to offer. Email campaigns build know, like, and trust, they show your value, and they keep your business relevant to the busy lives of your leads and customers.

Email campaigns also help you keep track of who your customers are, who your leads are, and all pertinent information. They help you learn what your potential leads want and need and expect.

They help you upsell and build loyal, steady customers.

They help you identify top prospects for later dialogue with.

So, how do you get people to sign up for an email campaign, or a mailing list? It's time to learn about the concept of the funnel, first developed by Russell Bronson.

Funneling leads to email campaigns from your physical storefront, website, and social media.

At your physical store, you could simply have a sign-up sheet. You can also use raffles or other give-aways to gather permission to share deals and news. You can use your social media page to encourage people to opt-in.

But the heart of your funnel is your website. Your website is your go-to space in your funnel. Your store should send people to your website, your presence in your community should send people to your website, your social media should send people to your website---starting to see how the funnel works?

You need to be ready for when people click to your website. Right out the gate, you should be offering them something of value in exchange for their email address. It can be an informative pdf or video, or email series chock full of relevant information. If you have a newsletter that you release on a regular basis (weekly, monthly, bimonthly), you can invite people to sign up for that.

Checking how many people click on to your website then decide to not opt in to your exchange of valuable content for email address can provide you valuable information about your business.

However you go about it, your goal is to build know, like, and trust by giving them something that they value. And continuing with that with all further communication.

So, everything leading to the website which leads to people being inspired to exchange their contact information for some great content or discount. The funnel expands from there, but this is a good beginning overview from which to work this week.

Take some time today to review your website. Also take some time to observe others' website landing pages, and funnels from social media to website to the giving away of content or deals. Feel free to make some observations in your journal.

Wednesday: Plan Out Your Funnel

Pick an event, holiday, or sale that is on your calendar within the next 2 months; if you don't have anything, go back to months 2-4, to work on this aspect of running your business.

Based on that event, we are going to create a funnel for you to build your campaign around. Your funnel can be as simple or as complex as you have time for. The key is remembering your soft skills from week 1, the need for authenticity, and machine gun marketing tactics from month 3.

Here is a sample funnel for a small business that sells mala beads from a website and sells out of a yoga studio owned by a friend. Joan, who sells the beads, has researched and identified her target audience: women in their 30s-60s who have generally been practicing yoga over 5 years. In listening to customers, she's realized that a lot of women buy them as birthday gifts for their mothers or daughters. She has started tracking birthday data of her customers.

She doesn't know the birthday of the mothers of her customers, but, she practices the techniques of a good visionary and healthy life as outlined in this book, and she comes up with a new idea.

She decides to generate an ad campaign around the idea of giving a gift to a special, respected woman on their own birthday. She knows her customer base is generous and likes to be creative. She thinks even if they don't do it that way, they might buy some beads to give on the actual birthday of their mother or important mentor figure.

So, she sets up an automated email campaign to be triggered a month before birthday of her existing customer list, and for it to operate the first year of every new customer.

She decides to do it a month early because her products usually take about 2 weeks to ship. She knows she has to have compelling ideas for an email, because she really likes her clients, and doesn't want to seem gimmicky. It's about taking the excitement and happiness of the customers who've shared how it felt to give them to moms or daughters, and sharing it.

She also likes her idea because she won't have to generate any ads, and it gives her some opportunity to test some ideas for a Mother's Day special next year, when she has some money allocated for an ad campaign in her yearly budget.

She knows she needs to generate copy for 3 emails. One, a month out. One, 2 weeks out, and one on their birthday. She's decided it will not need a special landing page and she can just send people straight to her online store with a discount code, but she wants to take notes for what works for a landing page ad copy, and a Facebook campaign for that upcoming Mother's Day campaign. Joan decides to trigger a text for those who click through the email to her online store. Because of the size of her client list, and that the birthdays are spaced out enough, she thinks she has time to personally respond if the clients text back, but she knows if her business grows as she plans, that she will have to redesign the campaign once she hits a certain number of customers. She blocks out time in her calendar for 6 months from now to redesign. If she doesn't need to redesign at that point it won't be too hard to fill that block in her calendar.

When she's drawing it out on a sketchpad, it looks like this:

New Client → get birthday on intake form
(double check all client b-days in CRM)

1st email — 2 links to landing page

Sense of urgency?   landing page
                                     pics of beads

                                     links to other
                                     deals/info
                                     [if clicked, text follow-up]
                                           next day
2nd email — link to landing page special product 1

              link to landing page special product 2
                             [if clicked, text
                                      follow up]
    sense of urgency?

3rd email — last chance! Expires Tmw

      short, pics of beads, 1 link to landing page
                                [text follow up]

      Opt-in to another campaign

Your turn.

Get creative. Think about who already shops with you. Your best potential leads are going to have traits and values and habits of behavior in common. Be realistic about what you can accomplish. Joan tries to keep hers as simple as possible because she is new to this skillset.

If you can't make it part of a longer vision like Joan does with testing ideas and language for a Mother's Day sale, that's okay. That skill will come with repetition of generating automated email campaigns and observing how they do with your leads and customers.

This is probably going to take more than a day. Go ahead and keep up with the daily reading if you can, as it will help you spark ideas and give you more information that you can utilize in developing your funnel.

Thursday: Creating a Landing Page on Your Site for Your Campaign

Most of the time your email campaign needs a landing page on your website for your customer to click through to.

Having a specific landing page emphasizes what is special and valuable about the deal or promotion you are offering. It is well worth the time and effort to create unique landing pages for each campaign or promotion you run, as it subtly conveys the value of what you have to offer. It also helps you track data and trigger different types of follow-up.

Landing pages should follow all the rules of good website creation. You can use the checklist below, or find another expert in website building to consult for insight, ideas, and constructive criticism.

- o   Good visuals. Consider making a 30 second video.
- o   A clear and compelling description of the value that hits the pain points/needs of your target audience
- o   A sense of urgency or scarcity
- o   Testimonials

o Quick and easy purchase button or link

Take some notes for your landing page for your email campaign. Block off some time to create it, or delegate. Make sure you also have someone give you feedback and double check it.

If you don't feel quite ready to create a landing page, block off some time to research landing pages at a wide variety of companies. Or, you might consider hiring someone, or conducting some kind of trade to get a professional landing page.

Friday: Generating Ad Copy for Your Campaign

Depending on what type of promotion you are running, you may also need to invest in ads, fliers, mailers, etc.

Ad copy follows the same basic tenets of a good landing page. The main difference is the attention-grabbing element. Once someone has clicked through to a landing page, you have their attention. With ad copy, you have to grab and hold their attention.

That means the attention-getting element of the copy is the most important. Good ad copy, like a good campaign, stems from a thorough and nuanced understanding of the group you are trying to reach.

For example, Joan decides to run 3 different ads for her Mother's Day sale. She's created a special set of mala beads made of rose quartz. Below is the writing for the description of the beads on her sale landing page, as well as copy for 3 Facebook ads.

"Mother-love malas"

Rose quartz embodies the unconditional love of the Mother. Their energy softens self-judgment and frazzled nerves. My mother and I created these mala beads last year at her mother's house to celebrate 3 generations of motherhood.

Ad 1:
Our mothers give us the greatest gift of all—life and unconditional support. These mala beads embody the soothing energy of abiding love; a perfect symbol of appreciation for your mother!

Ad 2:
Motherhood is special. And moms, no matter how old their children are, stress and worry about their kids. Show your mom you love her just as unconditionally with these rose-quartz mala beads this year.

Ad 3:
Rose quartz embodies compassion and forgiveness—a trait mothers give but don't often give to themselves. My mother and I created these beads together because we are proud of the resilience, love, and laughter of our relationship, and we wanted to share that with you this year.

As the ads run, Joan monitors how effective each one is. She notices that Ad 3, which shares personal story was the most effective, and ad 2 was least effective. A week before the sale ends, she creates a new ad with a story about her grandmother and drops ad 2.

Depending on your business, you don't want to ignore the power of fliers and mailers. But Facebook and Google ads are a great way to quickly test the effectiveness of your copy, which can lead to more compelling fliers and mailers once you've used that testing to get a sense of what powerfully touches the needs and pain points of your target audience.

Schedule some time to create some ad copy for your campaign. Decide what spaces are the best to invest in distributing your ads. If you are used to only using Facebook to share promotions, consider taking the opportunity to invest a little in running a Facebook ad campaign. It will only help you learn about how to best articulate what is great and special about your company.

And—if ad copy is taking too big a bite of new skills, just get creative and imagine what you might do, even if your hands are full with your new funnel and email campaign, it is worth it to spark your creativity and take that small first step of envisioning some potential ad copy. It won't go to waste.

WEEK 3
LEVEL UP YOUR AUTOMATED ONLINE PRESENCE FOR THE UPSELL AND RETENTION

Monday: Build Your First Campaign; Stacking

Stacking is a tried and true method of closing the sale. It is a form of overvaluing the product you want to sell by 'stacking' other offers onto it. For example, if you are selling a weight loss course, you might "stack" a cookbook, a guide for eating out, and an at-home workout pdf as freebies they get when they sign up for the course. In the last example, Joan stacked a different offer at the end of her 3rd email.

Of course, to stack, you must have something to stack with. Pdfs, handouts, and informational videos make excellent items to stack onto the product you are selling. You can also use cross-promotion to "stack" a great deal on a product from a business your network if you can work out a good trade with your fellow business owner. For example, if you are running a promotion on pounds of coffee, you could stack a 30% off coupon for a dozen cookies from the bakery next door.

Stacking overvalues your product and conveys to people that they are going to get a great deal if they make the purchase.

Whatever you stack onto your promoted product, you need to ensure that it is quality and professional. Over time, you will generate a set of materials that you can use and reuse. Take some time to brainstorm some things you could create to stack onto your product. Then block out time across the next month to start creating them.

Tuesday: Build Your First Campaign; Visuals

Today, we're returning to the look and feel of the emails you are building for your automated campaign.

As we all know, visuals do much of the work of closing the sale. If you aren't used to using technology, it can feel a little intimidating to start adding visuals to the campaign. But it is well worth the effort, and like all skills, you will improve over time (or, you will be able to delegate as your business expands).

Your visual must be simple, eye-catching, and relevant to the content of the email. For instance, if you have testimonials in your email, you might get permission to use a picture of the person giving the testimonial, either a simple professional face shot, or one of them using your product or service. If your email shares some of your personal story, like Joan's Mother's Day campaign does, you might consider sharing a photo that represents that story. Joan used a picture of her and her mother working at her grandmother's table in her campaign. You can include a professional, high-resolution photo of your product. You can embed a YouTube video. You can also keep it simple, and embed your company logo, and use a signature block with a photo of yourself at the close, which emphasizes authenticity and a sense of connection between yourself and the email recipient.

Take a moment to brainstorm what an effective image or photo might be for your campaign. Try not to get too elaborate or start to invest in an idea that would simply take too much time. First reps through a new skill or practice should be simple and time-effective.

Wednesday: Build Your First Campaign; Email Subject and First Sentence

The sender, content, and tone of the email subject and preheader are what readers use to decide whether or not to open the email. Today we are going to give an in-depth look at the subject line and preheader of your email campaign.

While the goal is to encourage people to open the email, a secondary and still important goal is to create brand awareness. So, don't be discouraged by your return rate. Remember that building an impression of a new brand takes time and patience.

Let's start with the subject line. A good tactic is to treat the subject heads across the campaign as an arc. Often people build the sense of urgency (i.e., '24 hours left!') in the subject line of the final email in a series).

Another good tactic, particularly in the first email, is to ask a question (i.e., 'hungry for new experiences?' for a promotion on a class they might not have tried before). Your question should directly address the pain point or needs of your target audience. Be careful to avoid overused words like "tired" "hurry" etc.

It is a trial and error process to find what keywords work with your audience. You have to stay involved and humble and willing to observe what works and what doesn't.

Subject lines also require balance between being "eye-catching" and being informational. You want it to have some emotional impact, but not be so vague they don't have a clear reason to open. Specificity of what's in the email is important.

There also isn't a hard and fast rule about the length. Generally, you want to keep it as short as possible, particularly with the rise of people using their phones to check email. The current industry standard is 41 characters, but again, that is not a hard and fast rule.

The essential takeaway here is to take a trial and error approach to finding what key words and approaches work with your people. Software such as MailChimp provide excellent tools for developing a sophisticated approach to crafting subject lines, preheaders, and emails based on your email lists.

Preheader text is the first line of text that shows up following the subject line of the email. Email providers have different rules on how much text shows, so it is important to get a sense of the number of people on your list that use the different email providers to help you shape your email campaigns.

As your skills grow—or if you are hiring a pro—you can hide preheader text from the body of the email, but make sure you double check that it isn't accidently showing! Hiding preheader text is great if your email is almost all visuals.

Most often, you can think of the preheader text as an extension of the subject line. You can use it as a call to action, or to pique curiosity so that they click open the email to read on.

You can also use the preheader to appeal to different audiences, depending on how sophisticated you want to get with your automated campaign (something you can return to in later campaigns).

Also, I want to take a minute to mention that by law you must have an unsubscribe button so that people may opt out.

It can be a little overwhelming at first to navigate subject lines and preheaders, where there are no hard and fast rules, just concepts to balance and the need for patience with trial and error.

Take a moment to look through your testimonials, Yelp reviews, customer notes, 'About Us' page, etc. Select some key words that show up a lot, and experiment with creating some subject lines and preheaders that use those key words.

You might also consider making 2 lists and 2 sets of subject lines and preheaders, so that way you can test which group gets a greater response. That will give you some words and concepts to build on in future campaigns.

Thursday: Testing, Double-checking, Gather the data

Before you launch your email campaign, at the very minimum, take a day or two break from it, then re-read it and check all the links before you launch. Taking a day or two away helps you have a fresh perspective for that final look before launching.

Once, I launched an email campaign without looking it over. I was crunched for time and decided to just go ahead and launch. Well, the links that took to landing page weren't working. I sat for 2 days, checking on my notifications to come in on a sale being closed (when sales come in I get notified).

Nothing was connecting, because the links were broken. The whole chain was broken because there was a broken link. All that effort I put into creating and launching 6 ads, building a landing page, and creating a funnel and copy for my email campaign was almost wasted because I got in a hurry at the end and didn't check the links. It's easy to get hasty, to think, 'well I've already looked at this thing 20 times, I'm not going to see anything, let me just launch it and move on.' But you should always reserve some care for details and fresh perspective for that final look. If you're the type that just can't see those kinds of errors in your own work, then hire or delegate the task to someone with proven ability to see the fine-grain detail to give it a final look.

Throughout this month, I've talked a little bit about running tests and gathering data on what works. When I'm running ad campaigns, my tactic is to launch 6 ads, find which one is having the most success, and close the other 5 and pour more resources into the ad that works.

With testing copy and gathering data, there are no hard and fast rules. Mostly it is about having an open mind, a willingness to learn about your people, and patience for failure and staying organized.

If you are completely new to email campaigns, you are probably already feeling overwhelmed. I recommend beginning at least with ads and emails to start to gather data, even if it feels like too much. It will save you time in the long run to develop this skill at the same time as you develop the skill of creating an automated email campaign.

In addition to ad copy and key words, you can test the content and structure of your campaigns (i.e., maybe your people like emails to read like a letter; maybe they respond better if it is a series of images). You can also create test groups for what time of day or week you send the email, as well as the frequency.

Once you're starting to get beyond those skills of testing and gathering data, I recommend hiring a proven expert to help you take this to the next level.

Take a moment to look back to the day on ad copy and email subject line. See if you can develop 2 groups to test how key words or content work. Keep it simple, but take the time to practice testing—otherwise how will you improve? How else will you get a real feel for who you spark and how?

Friday: Launch Your Campaign

Are you ready to launch your campaign? Pick your launch date (remembering to plan in that last careful look), and congratulations and best of luck! I invite you to share your results in my Facebook group.

If you're not ready, that's okay. There was a lot to learn this month. Take today to work on what you need to, and set a deadline for yourself and set up, or refine, your plan for achieving your goal of launching that first campaign.

WEEK 4
OVERVALUING YOUR PRODUCT

Monday: Why It Matters

Marketing is a game of perception. That's why so many people are so uncomfortable with it, and avoid taking advantage of things like email campaigns and automation.

You can play the game of perception without being unethical. It is simply the company's responsibility to educate the public about who the company is, what they stand for, and what they do. More and more, customers want that education before they commit their dollars. As a small business owner, it is part of your job as the visionary to have a deep understanding of who your target audience is, what their thoughts and feelings are when it comes to what is relevant to your product or service, and to use that knowledge to create a plan for directly and honestly addressing those thoughts and feelings with your marketing campaign.

So, when I say, overvalue your product, I am talking about being willing to be realistic about human nature and the society we live in, not to take advantage of people, but to give the value of what you have to offer a chance to be heard by those who might benefit from spending money at your store.

Look back through the 5 companies you researched 2 weeks ago. Make some observations in the space below about how they create a perception of value around their services.

This week is more about sharing information to help you refine your ability to run a successful email campaign or promotion of any sort.

That way, those of you who need it, have time to finish the automated email campaign while still staying on-track with opening this book every day.

Tuesday: What It Means To Have a Sale or Give a Discount

When you walk into a mall, you will quickly notice that everyone is running some sort of sale or discount. No matter what kind of store, they are having some sort of sale or promotion, just to get you to walk in the door.

Having this sort of mindset, of sparking initial interest with a great deal is part of being the type of visionary that is skilled at accelerating their business.

Today, go to your Facebook page and see if you can make a change or adjustment to have your page better feature some sort of discount or deal. If you have time, and are finished your email campaign, apply this principle elsewhere—your storefront, your website homepage, etc.

As you get good at this, you are going to want to have some sort of sale or discount going at all times. Keep that in mind as you plan and percolate good ideas.

Wednesday: Rewarding Loyalty

We've talked about rewarding loyalty in month 4, week 2. It's an important aspect of overvaluing your product or service to your loyal customers.

Brainstorm some ideas below for an email campaign or other type of promotion you could launch that targets your loyal customers or rewards loyalty. For example, if you own a restaurant, for the week of your birthday or another occasion that makes sense based on your brand and mission, you could give everyone that comes in a coupon for 10% off their next visit.

After you've jotted down or researched potential ideas, look at your yearly calendar and block off time for setting up this new automated campaign of emails or texts specifically geared around rewarding loyalty.

Thursday: Sparking Leads

Your main effort on campaigns and promotions should be those that spark new leads. This requires blending many of the skills and automations we've worked through into one project or campaign: overvaluing, stacking, machine gun marketing, testing ad copy, funneling to landing pages, etc.

If you have a physical storefront, get a sense of who lives in the area and create fliers, mailers, or do a cross-promotion with another local business that targets what you understand about their interests and what might motivate them to try your store. Remember Tuesday—**entice with a great deal, set up your funnel wisely and keep building on existing funnels.**

If your storefront is digital, you can use Faceboook, Google, etc to create an ad campaign that sparks new leads, or you can inspire customers to refer you.

Either way, take some time to research who you can appeal to to spark new people to check out your business.

Friday: Continuing to Build the Funnel

Notice how this week ended up generating a lot of new ideas for launching new campaigns? There are 3 main areas to split your focus as the visionary when it comes to getting new people in the door: having an enticing storefront, motivating current customers to return, and motivating new people to check you out.

Now that you have the basics and a sense of how to generate new ideas, look ahead on your calendar and begin building a rhythm around major events or sales in terms of creating ideas for a campaign, building the campaign, and launching it. Use the calendar skills we've practiced to start to experiment with, and fine-tune how you use your time to best effect.

MONTH TEN
RESEARCHING YOUR MARKET AND YOUR COMPETITION

Last month was intense. We built on staying up to speed by adding automation, reps, and a seasonal rhythm for generating marketing campaigns to get people in the door, to get eyeballs on your page.

I wanted to start with the action of generating ideas and building marketing rhythm into your calendar before taking a deeper dive into understanding your ideal customer and your competition. I did this deliberately, to emphasize the importance of action, and how there is always more to learn, but you can't let feeling like you don't know enough yet or are uncomfortable, impede you from implementing.

So, if you're still working on that first automated email campaign and the first parts of your funnel, that is perfectly okay and even expected. The month, we go further in-depth into understanding your target demographic that way as you expand you will have a clear system for knowing who you want to reach now, what they want, and how to reach them (as well as to build knowledge and experience on reaching those around you that you haven't yet figured out how to reach).

We also start to build automation for staying up-to-date in your industry, community, and the business world in general. This might seem unnecessary, or a lot of extra work for nothing, but if you automate it, and keep it simple, then it will have major lasting benefits for your company. Remember, as the business owner, part of having the vision is knowing what else is out there. This helps you spark your creativity and stay relevant.

WEEK 1
UNDERSTANDING YOUR IDEAL CUSTOMER

Monday: Why It Matters

There are a few ways to approach developing a thorough understanding of who you are trying to reach and help with what your business offers.

Your potential leads are out there. First, you have to understand where they are and what they need.

Then, you experiment with learning how to communicate with them. That's marketing.

So, who are your potential leads? What kind of people are they? Having a grasp on this takes some real ability with the imagination, which is why I've left this to month 10. At this point with all the reflecting and creative work we've been doing, your imaginative skills should be ready to navigate getting a firm grip on who you are trying to reach with your business.

This week we talk about avatars, pain points, and who is in your neighborhood. An avatar, as we cover more in-depth later, is a sketch of your ideal customer. You can use a real person that you know, or you can create an 'ideal sketch' of that avatar. As your company expands, you will expand the number of avatars you are working with. So, what good are avatars? They help you focus your mind and imagination with your marketing content and tactics to maximize your ability to reach people who resonate with that avatar.

Take today to reflect on the patterns and qualities you notice in your current loyal customer base. Focusing your mind on this will start to feed information to your brain so that it is more ready to do the work this week, so don't skip or skimp on this.

Tuesday: Look Up Information about Who Lives in Your Neighborhoods

As the owner of a small business with a physical storefront, it is important to have an understanding of your immediate community, as well as how various neighborhoods and groups of people interact within your vicinity. For example, if you own a coffeeshop located next to a yoga studio, the folks driving to their cubicle job looking for a cup of joe in the morning are one demographic, and the people attending am, lunch, or evening yoga classes are another demographic.

You can gather information about the groups of people that either live near, drive through, or regularly visit your area from 2 sources. One way, like in the example above, is from observing the other shops and what types of people are regular customers.

The second is taking the time to hop online, research, and compile the demographics data for those who live in the neighborhood, and any other pertinent neighborhoods based on the layout and personality of your town or city.

There are companies you can pay for this service. If you hire out for marketing services, this type of research will often be part of what you're purchasing. It depends on your company, your time, your budget, and your strengths and weaknesses whether or not you want to hire out or manage this yourself. Be mindful though that your time is the most valuable of everybody's, your skillset the most unique and valuable, and you aren't really saving yourself money if you're pouring your effort into menial tasks you could pay someone else to do. Take for example, if a lawyer made all his own copies and filings. If that was 5 hours of his week, that's a significant net loss.

So you can hire this out, you can pay for software that finds and compiles this data, or you can use free services to find and compile this data. You don't want to just rely on your field of vision of who drives by or shops nearby, because that is not going to give you a fully accurate picture.

The Census Bureau has a search engine here. They have topics you can search by, as well as by area or zip code.

Some data you will want to compile about your neighborhoods:

o   Average income
o   Age
o   Gender
o   Race
o   Married, single, household size

Take some time to browse the Census Bureau website, as well as reflect on what the best option for you is going to be in terms of whether you invest your time or your dime on gathering this data. Block out some time in the future for either doing the research, or assimilating the research.

Take notes.

Wednesday: Other Questions To Ask about Your Ideal Customer

Gaining a sense of your ideal customer is as much an art as it is a science. Like much of the other skills and concepts taught in this book, you have to take a trial and error approach, and you have to learn to apply principles and concepts, not merely check off a to-do list and leave it at that.

One of the key principles to apply to developing an avatar is to make your avatar as human as possible. Developing your imagination is an essential component of being a visionary and skilled at accelerating your business. This reality is probably the most apparent when it comes to developing that avatar.

Many in the business world recommend having an avatar as an individual, an imaginary (or real) character with a face and a very detailed profile of their life. In my experience, it depends on your business and your own personality whether or not that approach is going to be effective for you. It is certainly a good beginner step for those who are uncomfortable or unskilled at using their imagination and soft skills to really get to know the types of people that make ideal leads for your product or service.

Whether or not you have an individualized face or a general set of traits, part of the art comes in balancing between generalizing across groups of people and leaving room for the uniqueness of every individual.

Here is a list of questions to ponder as you work on your sketch of your avatar:

o What is her career? What is her work environment like?
o What communities or organizations is he involved in?
o How does she spend her free time? What are her priorities or goals in life?
o What mistakes does he regularly make? What are her blind spots in life?
o What is his attitude toward spending money?
o What are the big struggles or hurdles in life?
o How does family play a role in his life?
o When and how does she use technology? Social media?

You will want to craft a few more questions pertinent to what you offer, as well as revise some of these to be more relevant to your business and location.

Start to ponder these questions and write down some thoughts. At this stage we are still 'throwing spaghetti at the wall' so just throw and don't worry about accuracy or what sticks.

Thursday: Understanding Their Needs and Pain Points in General

Once you've got a sense of the big picture of your avatar's personality, life, and lifestyle, you can start to sketch in an intimate understanding of their needs and pain points. It's important to start with a neutral, big-picture look in order to guard against overgeneralizing, stereotyping, overlooking something, or making some sort of egregious assumption. Starting with the demographics of your neighborhood, then building a sense of who they are, then transitioning to pain points or needs is a solid, tested process for giving your creativity and visionary skills opportunity for that creative insight. Having a system and taking the time to carefully apply yourself to each step is essential to making space for creativity, and space for creativity is what is going to make your company stand out.

So, now that we've covered that, let's zoom in on creating that fine-grain understanding of their needs and pain points.

Pain points are what your business solves for in their life, so you need to be able to understand it in the way that *they* think through it.

The reason people recommend putting a face and a name to your avatar is because it helps you have empathy for them, and that empathy triggers a deeper level understanding of their situation that helps you better reach them with your branding. When you've let your imagination loose and really imagined little details about their house, their car, how they do their hair or joke with their friends, it triggers your empathy and creativity and brings it to bear in designing the language you use to reach them about the value and benefit of your product or service.

So if you were a bit half-hearted or uncertain in using your imagination yesterday to think through your avatar, take some time to daydream right now.

Once you feel that you've really connected with your avatar, reflect on the following and take notes.

Imagine your avatar's morning. Their commute to work. Their work day. What they do in their personal time in the evening, weekend, and holidays. How do they use their phone? How do they interact with family? Friends? Social media? What other scenarios in their life really matter to them? Which ones are relevant to you? Try to let go of previous assumptions about which ones are relevant and see where your imagination leads you.

Really take the time to let your imagination roam and create details.

Once you feel 'immersed' in your avatar's world, start to think about what feels overwhelming to them in their world. What in their life are they using to cope? This can and is a mix of good and bad things.

Also think about what your avatar doesn't notice about herself that other people do. (i.e., she always double-books her Friday nights; she misses important deadlines; she talks a lot about vacations or learning a new skill but never follows through; she has an awful temper; etc etc)

What is the thing that your avatar worries about, stresses over, or avoids completely?

What does your avatar dream about for his life, and how far is it from the reality? What is the cause of the gap between reality and dream?

Friday: Incorporating Your Avatar Profile into Your Other Systems

Let's start today with a little housekeeping.

First, you might have more than one avatar. Most businesses expand by either developing products or services that reach different people, or by developing their marketing to get their product to reach different types of people. You might need a couple avatars now, you might not. But either way as your business expands you need to stay mindful of change, both to your main avatar and to what other types of people or pain points are going to be potential avenues for you.

Second, I cannot emphasize enough the importance of an open mind. As I've been training you in all along, you've got to watch out for your own blind spots and assumptions, and you've got to keep creating space for your imagination to have room to run and spark creative insights or ideas.

Part of keeping an open mind is being willing to engage in a trial-and-error process for both developing your avatar and developing how your brand reaches people. Part of the trial and error means listening to your customers, leads, and staff, as we've covered in other sections.

The other part of the trial and error process, which is the main focus for today, is how you incorporate your avatar into your marketing systems, customer service systems, and staff training systems.

Alright, now that we've covered the fundamentals, let's talk about incorporating avatars into marketing.

Connecting with your avatar should be the first step of building a marketing campaign plan.

Some people like to storyboard. Some like to hold imaginary conversations with their avatar. Me, I like to brainstorm with my marketing team. Creativity doesn't have a one-size-fits-all firestarter. While at this point, you might have more familiarity with how to set the stage for your best ideas, you still want to keep an open mind and experiment til you find something solid, then lock it into place with repetitions repetitions repetitions.

Pull out your calendar. When are you scheduled to develop that next marketing campaign? Build in this step of connecting with your avatar into your planned use of time.

Honing in on their pain points creates your keywords and refines your brand.

It's been awhile since we've talked about brand and keywords. Incorporating your insights about your avatar into your word choice on your website, social media, and brand statement should be in a feedback loop with your development of ad copy and marketing campaigns.

Testing the success of ad copy should feed back into your 'image' of your avatar.

You want to keep your avatar image simple, after you've developed the big picture and work toward refining at the fine grain level. As you develop ad copy and key words and your brand, keeping track of what fails or what works should feed back into a troubleshoot session on the realism and simplicity of your sketch of your avatar.

Brainstorm how you can incorporate these insights into your marketing and evaluating processes.

Once you've done that, add your next steps to your weekly focus agenda, and any other space on your calendar that it needs to go.

WEEK 2
MARKET TO YOUR AVATAR

Monday: Developing Ad Copy

This week, we are going to hone in on developing ad copy for the avatars we created last week.

The best strategy I have found for ad copy is to launch 5-6 different ads, observe their success, cancel the ones that aren't working, and double down on what is getting clicks.

Sometimes my 5-6 different ads target different avatars with the sale. Sometimes my 5-6 different ads take different approaches to connecting with the pain point of my potential leads. Sometimes my 5-6 different ads take different tacks for creating urgency. Sometimes, it is a combination of 2 or more of those.

As we build this skill, let's keep it simple. Today, I want you to look ahead on your calendar and identify what marketing campaign we will be creating ad copy for. If you don't have an upcoming campaign, review and do more research on how to automate regular campaigns. Then, develop your timeline and vision for your next one.

Start to take notes or generate ideas. Right now, no limits, just get whatever pops in your head onto paper. Unfetter your creativity. We'll refine this week.

Tuesday: Testing Multiple Ads with Multiple Types of 'Spark'

When I was opening my business, one of my mentors showed me guerrilla marketing (low-cost marketing) and machine gun marketing (driving traffic from different channels). When I was opening up, I gathered all my friends to do different types of guerilla and machine gun marketing. We printed 15,000 fliers and walked through the neighborhood, putting fliers on all the cars we see. For 3-4 weeks we blasted with fliers. Then, I made doorhangers and printed 15,000 door fliers. Then, we made postcards. We put postcards in all the stores in the neighborhood. On their cars, in the stores.

Then we set up a booth right in front of the studio and handed out fliers to walk-by traffic. Then we updated our Google listing to make sure people could find us there.

We made a press release (usually free) talking about how important this service this is in the neighborhood, trying to welcome ourselves in.

We made free posts on Craigslist (update them weekly because they expire), so when people search key words, our post shows up via the search engine.

With me using guerilla and machine gun marketing, I was able to accelerate my growth by 400%.

Nowadays in terms of these 2, an effective tool is to advertise in different Facebook groups that Facebook offers as well as on WhatsAp, LinkedIn, and Twitter.

Combining these techniques will generate fast growth for your business.

Wednesday: Create Ad Copy To Overvalue Your Company

Your ads should clearly address the pain point and offer a solution. You can study any and all advertisements out there for materials and insight on this. How you agitate the pain point and offer the solution should be built on the values, language, and character of your brand.

Your ad copy, in addition to generating leads who click to the landing page for a particular promotion or campaign, should also routinely give stuff away for free, and inspire people to 'become a member' whatever that means for your unique business.

A common tactic for this is free webinars. One that I like to use because I have a physical store and sell the skills of my highly trained staff, is having a special event for either new leads, or loyal regulars, depending on the season and the overall goal. The event is free, but there are a limited number of spaces, which creates a sense of urgency. At the event, either I give a speech, or I train my staff to share the special promotion or deal that I am offering.

Maybe you're not ready to get that complex and involved in the layers of your funnel. That's okay. But you still need to be creating ad copy that overvalues your company. It can be as simple as funny tweets or re-posting relevant videos or links. It can be a newsletter or series of videos. It can be simple advice or raffles. Whatever it is, you need to have it built in to every season, every month, to overvalue your company in the eyes of your leads.

Pull out your calendar and make a plan for building this into your rhythm. Make sure that this builds back in to your funnel, that it has a clear purpose and place in the overall vision.

Thursday: Assess Your Process

These past 2 weeks we've developed some new strategies and principles for developing ad copy and approaching how you connect with potential leads. It's time to take a step back and assess.

What was easy? What skills did you bring to the table that made this project go more smoothly?

What was a challenge? Where were your skills weakest?

How are you measuring success? What is your plan for failure with ads? What is your plan for observing how the campaign goes?

You might want to take a few days to think this over, and plan for your next weekly focus meeting to finish completing this, even if you read the whole day right now. This kind of thinking you want to let simmer.

Now that you have a clearer sense of your strengths and weaknesses, and a clearer sense of how you plan to troubleshoot the campaign to maximize success, it's time to make some tweaks and adjustments for the next time you go through this process of developing ad copy and a marketing campaign.

The first thing to tweak is, how good a job did you do double-checking your work? Both the writing and imagery and plan as well as links and website landing page? If that wasn't an automated, straightforward part of your process, take the time now to figure out how to make some small improvements for next time.

Okay, now that we've got that in hand, let's move to strengths and weaknesses.

First, ask yourself honestly, are you going to be able to dedicate yourself to making improvements in your ad copy such that your conversion rate continues to increase toward its maximum potential?

It's okay if that isn't your strength, or if you just don't have the time. It's one thing to be afraid and avoid out of fear, anxiety, or unmanaged stress. It's another to acknowledge honestly that it just isn't your bag. If that's the case, then you need to zoom out to your big picture, your 3-year plan and goals, and find a way to rearrange the flow of money such that you can hire someone to manage this aspect of your business. I think it's important for every small business owner to go through this process, even if they hand the task off, it's important to have experienced the process so you can ask intelligent questions and have a good process for evaluating what you are getting from a hire or subordinate's work. Even if you hand it off, you are still in charge of the brand, the goal, and the awareness of the humanity of your target market.

Alright, so you've decided to keep building your skills. Looking back over the past 2 weeks as a whole, as well as what you've observed about what didn't work, do some free-writing observation.

Now, looking at your resources, what is the best, most efficient way to develop the skills that you need to increase your success with ad copy?

Pull out your calendar and build your plan.

Friday: Train Your Staff/Catch Up

First, write out each step in your process of moving from avatar, pain points, through launching and assessing a marketing campaign.

Now, next to each step, write an estimate for about how much time each step requires, to include which steps can be done in the same day and which need a few days for that creative simmer.

Now that you have a map of the big picture, what steps can be delegated? How can you take advantage of staff to improve the process?

What skills or abilities will staff need to be trained in to start to automate this process and maximize its ability to succeed?

Who on your staff has potential for a leadership role? Create a plan for including them in the process of giving them room to grow within your company.

For those of you without staff, take today to catch up on anything that you haven't been able to get to yet.

WEEK 3
MAINTAINING & UTILIZING YOUR CRM DATABASE

Monday: Why It Matters

As we've emphasized all along, automation leads to huge gains in terms of the time you input into marketing and sales and your reach and return

And when it comes to reaching those potential leads, being able to wield your CRM data with skill is essential.

Today I want you to refresh yourself on the tools your CRM has when it comes to examining lead and customer data.

Also, do a big picture assessment—when do you look at your database? Is it an automatic part of

- o Accounting and billing
- o Building marketing campaigns for potential leads
- o Upselling customers
- o Determining who your loyal customers are and what makes them happy
- o Determining who out there wastes your time or abuses the system
- o Refining your avatar
- o Having a fine-grain, automated process of evaluating, refining, and expanding your funnel

Several of the things on the list work hand-in-hand, but I wanted to separate them out for you. Look at this list, what is your biggest priority for improving automation? Create your plan for improving the efficiency of your use of CRM in that aspect of your business.

Tuesday: Using and Integrating Different Software

What is your current software priority? Is it Instagram? Google Calendar? MailChimp? A client scheduling software? OpenTable? An accounting software? What are the top 2 software priorities for your business right now? How does the CRM you are considering align with that?

I got PM software in 2005. When I first got the software, it was really ahead of its time. It had email automations. It had text messaging. It had voice broadcast where you could send a blast to all your clients or prospects (voicemail). As time went on, for some reason they dropped the ball and stopped updating the software. So now, in 2019, it's outdated. Text messages are still there, but it's not updated. I can't have an isolated conversation like other programs offer and that I know I need for my business. After a text blast, there is no way for them to reply.

That 2005 software also has a really outdated check-out process. Back in 2005, there were no other options available in terms of checkout process online, people understood how much time it was going to take to finish checking out on those programs—there wasn't anything faster. Nowadays, people are really busy and they don't want to spend a lot of time checking out online buying a product or service. So it's important that the software you're using has ease of use for customers. The simpler it is to check out, the more sales you will make.

The software I currently have doesn't have that option. It takes at least 10 clicks to make a purchase, wherease nowadays there are 1 or 2 clicks tops to make a purchase. So what I had to do, is, I had this software, and I needed to redirect my clients to another software that is easier to use. I purchased and set-up another software for the checkout process.

Take some time today to research and mull over where your current software is lagging, and what other programs exist that you could integrate to improve the experience for customers and leads.

Wednesday: Website Integration

Your CRM should help you observe who goes to what pages on your website. To that end, you want to have landing pages for every different type of service, and every different type of sale. Take some time today to assess how you can add some more flesh to your website so you can get a finer-grain look at who is looking at what. From there, you want to build the funnel of follow-ups for when eyeballs land on the page.

Schedule it, knock it out.

Thursday: Train Your Staff

As you integrate a new software into your system, you need to use your best practices from the month on staff training to ensure your staff know what they need to know for using the software to best advantage. If you don't have any staff, take the time to train yourself thoroughly.

Take today to cook up your plan for staff training. Refer back to month 3 for a refresher before creating your plan for making sure your staff has the support and information they need to succeed.

Friday: Reflect, Reorient, Strategize

Return to your 1- and 3-year goals. How does this new information on marketing shift those goals? Is your plate too full? Are you starting to get a sense of how much time a campaign takes, from idea genesis to implementation, to troubleshooting and assessment? Step back and look at your big picture. Be realistic about what needs to shift around, and be clear-eyed in terms of tying these new marketing practices to measurable, long-term goals for your business.

WEEK 4
KNOW THY COMPETITION

Monday: Why It Matters

Your business lives and thrives in a complex ecosystem of culture, politics, and competition. I don't believe business is a zero-sum game, but to truly give your company an edge, you need to have a system for staying on top of what is going on, not only in the ecosystem of people who might need or want your product/service, but also in terms of who else is in your industry, whether or not they are direct competitors.

Knowing your competition helps you keep your creativity fresh and current as well as helps you ensure your brand maintains its distinctive personality.

People have a finite amount of time, attention, and money, so I like to divide up my understanding of my competition into 3 categories:

What businesses are located near mine. Often, this group is the least competitive and the most symbiotic. As we talked about in week 1 of this month, a neighborhood or shopping area often supports and brings each other up, or drags each other down. When you think about the businesses located near you, think about how you can better pull together, encourage, and inspire each other to make your block or neighborhood a real draw. It may take work and seem like a lot of unnecessary personal politics at times, but in the long run it really pays off.

If you don't have a physical storefront, get creative on working out what your unique ecosystem of symbiotic relationships is. It could be a professional group, a local group, or some other mix of entrepreneurs that suits your personality and your business.

What businesses offer similar products/services. This group is further divided into small businesses and national chains. You want to have and maintain a thorough understanding of who else offers what, and how what you offer compares, both in terms of distinctions and in quality/price point. How can you distinguish yourself without understanding what you are distinguishing yourself from?

Keeping an eye on businesses in the same field also helps you keep track of what is appealing to customers, both in terms of product and in terms of marketing techniques. It helps you to stay on top of trends and changes, and perhaps even be the one who innovates the next change. Knowing how your strengths and weaknesses match up gives you talking points in your marketing strategies.

Businesses that are in different industries but are relevant to you. For example, if you run a restaurant, all the businesses that compete for your food budget, or the politics that affect pricing, or food trends that sweep across the country can all have an impact on your business. Or, companies that host websites, such as WordPress, Wix, SquareSpace, or companies that offer food delivery, or grocery stores. You need to have your finger on the pulse of related industries that impact yours.

The other component of this group is watching for the leaders in marketing trends or innovating products or services, refer to the section on networking for a refresher on systems for gathering information on this group.

When researching these groups, ultimately it is your vision & goals that dictates what questions you ask as you make observations and notice patterns.

<u>Tuesday: Local Competition and Connections</u>

Take a few minutes to list your top 3-5 local competitors.

- How do they market?
- What does their website & social media presence look like?
- What do their reviews say?
- Are they listed on Google?
- Who spends money at their shop?
- Have they grown in the last 5 years? If so, why? IF not, why?
- What do you know about the business owners? The staff?

Take a few minutes to list the top 3-5 nearby companies (or companies that people in your network run). Answer the same questions about them.

What other questions might be worth asking about these companies?

Now it is time to use your imagination, creativity, and knowledge.

With the first group, use your skills to see what your observation, study, and imagination can create in terms of new ideas or insights for your business.

With the second, it is the same, but also adding, how might you cross-pollinate, or share resources?

Develop a plan and implement.

Wednesday: Researching People in your Industry

Now, do the same with 3-5 companies in your company across the States or internationally. Take the time to observe, gather information in the domains you've been developing your skills in. Be sure to take your time to observe neutrally before switching gears to imagination and idea generation. It's not about getting to an idea quickly, or getting to as many ideas as possible. It's about being careful and thorough so that the best insight hits that meets your current needs or problems.

Here are a list of research questions or things to make observations of:

- o What key words is their brand/about/mission statement built on?
- o Where else, and how do you see those key words deployed?
- o What does their social media presence look like? Engagement with that presence?
- o How does their website overvalue their products/services? What do they offer in exchange for your email and name?
- o How do they keep their website fresh so it stays highly ranked in Google, etc?
- o What pain points do they address? What do you notice about how they raise them, and how they claim to solve them?
- o How do they use social proof?

Thursday: Researching Success Stories

You want to have a plan for staying in the know on success stories, or what is new in the business world. Personally, I make a point to attend 1-2 conferences or conventions every year, as well as follow certain groups, with newsletters, on YouTube, Twitter, and Facebook groups. The trick here is to not let this eat up too much of your time. But the more you know about what your focus, priority, and current problem-set is, the easier it will be not to get lost in tangents.

Especially at this point, this one might seem like a lot to add to everything else you are now doing or learning. But, I think it is really important to have a plan in place for continuing to learn and stay tuned in to what is going on in the business world. It also does not have to take more than 10-15 minutes each week. Block off some time to find a good source for staying in regular conversation about what is going on in the business world. Maybe it's subscribing to a newsletter or podcast or LinkedIn group. Maybe it's committing to attend 1 conference a year. Maybe it's a networking group. Your call, but make the plan that fits your time, resources, and needs.

Friday: Putting It All Together

This system of observation and getting to know the competition doesn't necessarily have a software you can go out, research, compare options, and purchase. But that doesn't mean you can't automate how you go about staying on top of what's going on with your competition.

My recommendation is to set aside a small amount of time on a regular basis to catch yourself up. It really pays off to have an ongoing system of records of your observations. Perhaps you have a clever employee, friend, etc, who could help you design a really efficient recording system. Keeping tabs on how others are doing, both locally and otherwise, can help you develop an intuitive sense of market forces that could pay off in big dividends with some unforeseeable intuitive insight into accelerating your business. Knowing what people are doing, and how it is affecting their business, can also help you keep an objective understanding of your own operation.

Take a few minutes to look back over the month, and develop your plan for keeping the momentum moving forward on all these changes.

MONTH ELEVEN
AUTOMATION

Now that we've practiced all the basic actions and skills of generating and closing leads, these last two chapters we cover creating routines and rhythms around maintaining your website, social media presence, and generating new leads and sales.

All of it is about automation. But you have to be able to set yourself up for automation to operate smoothly. It's a matter of refining where your attention and focus goes, when.

There are daily tasks, weekly tasks, monthly, quarterly, seasonal, and yearly ones. The best thing you can do for your business is build a rhythm and a solid awareness around when you should be doing what. Now it is time to take everything you've learned about techniques for maximizing your reach through automation and walk you through how to manage the different parts of the process for managing business growth.

Just like you don't want to be brainstorming all the time til your mind crashes, you don't want to be so lost in taking care of all the little details that you don't have time to brainstorm and envision new creative ways to connect with people. And in between balancing those, you have to stay on top of *executing* new marketing campaigns all the while maintaining the excellence of your product or service. No wonder people avoid learning to automate and develop new ways of planning their time!

But, I can tell you from my own experience, it is so, so worth it. Like I've iterated all the way through this book, build your changes slowly. Consistent, slow change with solid planning and time management skills + the techniques in this book = accelerating your business like you would not have thought possible.

This chapter I 'graduate' you to no longer require a daily reading and task. This is meant to inspire and push you to keep everything going once you get to the end of the book. In this chapter, we walk through how stay organized and on top of your website/electronic presence, your automated interactions with leads and clients, as well as discussing your process, then we close with a more in-depth discussion of how to choose the right softwares to support your marketing and client interactions.

WEBSITE AUTOMATIONS

Review

Two months ago we talked about how every promotion should have a funnel: a landing page, ads, emails, fliers that motivate people to go to the landing page, and finally, stacking and overvaluing your offering such that leads sign up for the deal or promotion being offered on that landing page.

That funnel should be as automated as possible. That means you should be using software to manage and distribute your electronic ads, monitor responses to ads, and generate emails and texts in response to leads' actions on the landing pages for services, goods, and current promotions. Automated funnels mean you can have multiple ones going at a time and can focus your efforts more efficiently toward bringing more eyeballs to your company, and more leads converting to customers.

If you sell services, you should also be automating scheduling, with your schedule, clients' options for scheduling, and reminders for their appointments.

At this point, you should be feeling a lot better and more confident in your body and your health. If you've fallen off on eating well and exercising regularly, create a plan for reinvigorating those habits.

Two months ago, we practiced creating automated responses for generating leads and closing the sale. Go back and review the month now. The rest of this week we talk about how you can be most efficient with planning your time around continuing to practice creating these funnels, maintaining a professional website, and continuing to improve your electronic presence.

Daily Website & Social Media Tasks

Every day, you can optimize your visibility with your website and social media presence. You might have a set block of time each week or once a month for creating content, but you need to monitor comments and messages on a daily basis.

The best way to maximize SEO optimization, and therefore your ranking in search engines, is to have a daily or weekly blog (or video). There are always going to be people with a passion for reading about your passion. It does not have to be extensive, it does not have to be formal, it just needs to be authentic, relevant, and consistent.

Daily monitoring of comments means both responding to people as well as screening the autobots and ads. You need to make sure comments go through a vetting process. If possible, delegate this task. This is the kind of daily task that can easily eat up too much of your valuable time. Keep it on a timer, and save the best of your brainpower for the people in front of you, and your own projects that require creativity such as marketing campaigns, etc.

The daily tasks with checking comments can be something you multi-task on, something you delegate, or something you do at the end of your day or right before or after lunch. You don't want to be constantly checking—that wastes time. I check my comments during my morning work-out. For you, making a habit of doing this right before lunch might make more sense. Pick a time, make it consistent. Or, hand this off to one of your staff.

Weekly Website & Social Media Tasks

The other crucial weekly—or perhaps monthly, depending on your business—task is updating your events calendar on the website and social media platforms.

This regular update should also be sure to check the images and leadform captions, headlines, and taglines to make sure they are in keeping for where you are at in the year. This is an easy one to forget or overlook, and it can make you look really unprofessional and out of touch. For example, if it is approaching Valentine's Day and you still have a New Year's themed image on your homepage or website header, it is going to give the impression that you are disorganized and create a little bit of doubt or distrust in people's minds.

But, that is easy enough to avoid, if you block out a regular time to check your website over and make these quick little changes. Create your checklist and your rhythm and experiment with it til it is solid.

Updating your website could be an automatic step of developing and implementing new campaigns. You can also put 15 minutes in your calendar once a month, or every other week, to do a quick check-through of all the pages on your website and social media. This is also a task that is quite easily handed off to one of your staff.

Develop your plan for automating these routine tasks into your calendar. The goal is to minimize effort, balancing not being distracted by these tasks with not letting them slip off your radar.

Quarterly & Yearly Website & Social Media Tasks

Your quarterly, yearly, or biannual tasks are more of a look at the big picture, leaving the details for the daily/weekly view of your business.

With these tasks, it depends on you and your business how frequently you build them into your schedule.

Evaluate the effectiveness of your web pages and services. 4, 2, or 1 time a year, you should set aside time to make a big picture observation of which pages and which goods or services are performing the best, and which aren't. From that observation, you are going to want to spend some time evaluating or uncovering why certain things are doing well, and others aren't.

Looking at this on a regular basis helps you accumulate data that you can use in marketing, both in terms of how you connect with the lives of your leads, and in terms of what is a good deal, when.

It could be as simple as an outdated expiration date on a page lowering your conversion rate. It could be more complex. Start making this assessment a regular occurrence. I recommend 4x a year, because it is useful to look at this data seasonally for most businesses, but you personally might not have the time or energy to make big changes to your goods or services that often—especially if you're just getting started with software-driven marketing. Maybe you evaluate 4x a year, but only once a year do you really invest in changing up what you offer.

Add all the parts of this to your calendar.

Make a list of what you will look at, and what questions you will be asking. Do people on your staff need to be involved in evaluating? Maybe you need to add a staff meeting to the calendar around this evaluation of big picture data. Maybe getting some training or feedback needs to be part of your process for the first year or 6 months.

Observe and evaluate your reviews online. Maybe you have it automated as a daily/weekly task to respond to reviews, but you also need that big picture look. Add a bullet for including reviews in the evaluation event you just added to your calendar. Looking at them regularly helps generate marketing campaigns, target what needs fixing, and deepen your understanding of your brand in the minds of customers.

Stay on top of changes in technology and trends in website design and user experience. As websites change, people get used to the new features and feel of websites. Just like a sitcom show from 20 years ago is going to look and sound really outdated, a website from 5 years ago could feel the same, and that could potentially be a deterrent to people deciding to spend money with your company.

Now, if you haven't been much of one for websites up to this point, don't be discouraged! Remember, small steady changes.

Schedule into your calendar at least 1x a year, if not quarterly, to do some research/observation on what changes to website design and user experience have been occurring. You might include this as part of your regular research into your industry and your competition.

Website/Social Media Delegation & Research

As your business grows, it is as important to automate how you work with your staff as it is to automate software processes that interface with customers and leads. It depends on your personality, the specifics of your business as it stands right now, and your staff structure, how and what gets handed off. Today is about refreshing what principles and concepts to apply to determining what to delegate, and taking a moment to consider what in the material covered so far this week can be handed off to staff or others in your circle.

How much of the daily, monthly, and weekly website tasks can you hand off? How do you determine who is best suited for the job, in terms of logistics, temperament, skills, and interest? How will you train them? How will you keep an eye on the quality of work?

Which daily/weekly/monthly website/social media tasks do you feel cannot be handed off? Self-reflect. Is it out of a need for control, a fear of spending money, a feeling of isolation/nobody can help? If one of those emotions has a grip on your reason, take a few minutes to reflect on whether that emotion truly accurately reflects reality. Do you really need to make sure all the minutia is perfectly perfect?—How much time is it taking and what is it gaining you? What does the flow of money look like? What is the return on the value of your time and the other person's if you hand off this task? Can you do it as financially efficiently as possible? If it really isn't in the budget right now, can you look ahead to when you might have the money and put it into your planner?

Continuing Research. Software, websites, social media platforms are constantly evolving. How are you naturally and efficiently incorporating continuing to stay on top of changes into your workflow?

Troubleshoot Your Process

We've spent weeks now on websites, softwares, and social media and trying to get them as automated as possible so that you have a better reach, better chance of building rapport with leads, and better use of your time. Automating features on your website, social media, and taking advantage of the incredible tools of modern software is essential to accelerating your business. Now that we've spent weeks covering key principles and concepts, and worked through implementing some plans of action, where have you gotten stuck? What isn't working? Or, if it's all working smoothly, when and what is the next right step to take to keep building on the successes of accelerating your business?

If it helps, flip through the first 10 chapters for insight into where you are getting stuck and what principles, concepts, or action plans might best help you resolve where you are stuck [and remember, focused self-reflection and rest are both action plans that are often overlooked as useful when you get stuck]

AUTOMATING CONTACT WITH LEADS AND CUSTOMERS (CHATBOTS, TEXTING, ETC)

Review

Remember, wherever a lead or customer is in the decision-making process or process of interacting with you, you want that experience to be delegated to software as much as possible. As we talked about, this doesn't mean you lose the feel of the personal touch of your business. It just changes what that looks like.

This week is less about reviewing how to automate your time around this, and more about building on the work you did in month 9 in terms of outreach and automating outreach and the user experience for the mutual benefit of your company and your customers.

Develop your funnel for each service/product/promotion you offer

Each page should be segregated to a specific service. For example, say a yoga studio has 3 different types of class: stretching, hot yoga, vinyasa. Each service has its own page, so when leads search for it and land on that specific page, that lead gets to identify the specific service, so then you can automate targeting someone for that specific service that they searched. Separate pages allow you to know what they have interested in, and build automated contact around that interest.

After opting in, a lead should have ability to review info for that specific service. Once they make a purchase, purchase a class, auto direct to schedule page that only shows them the Bikram yoga class schedule.

Once they book their appoint, specific automation is set up: a text goes out to confirm appointment (if coming to class reply yes to confirm or reply no automate a response with a redirect link to reschedule.

Automatically update your calendar to confirm—most CRM programs will take care of this for you.

You can set up this kind of flow of responses with email, phone, & text messaging. For example, you might set up where the first part of the funnel is a text about their appointment. The automated response to no reply might be an email. The automated response to no reply to the email might be a phone call to confirm or reschedule the appointment. That's just one example, it's going to depend on you and your business how you blend automation and funnels across email, phone calls, and texts.

Say a new lead gets created from clicking to a landing page, but they did not purchase or book an appointment. You can have an automated text/email for this type of lead: 'welcome to xx,' just want to welcome you to our service, here's a little bit about us. Were you able to grab what you were interested in?' If they book or buy, the funnel triggers a stop. If they don't, it triggers next in sequence: hey thanks for reading the last email, here's another chance to receive xx deal on booking/buying. Third 'I'm really surprised you haven't taken me up on this offer, here's another chance to save on this campaign.

Carefully designed campaigns of this nature increase the chances of that lead making a purchase.

With technology and time, people are getting busier and busier. So they forget about your service, however interested they were when they clicked on the page, whatever their resolve to try it probably got lost in the bustle of life. When you remind them and reignite that interest, it increases the closing percentage. Win, win, win.

Test Your Automations 3 Times

Learn from my mistakes and make it a regular part of your marketing campaign process to test all your links and steps in your funnel to make sure they're doing what you want before you launch!

I was running a campaign, and I was spending a massive amount of money advertising a service. I thought the ads I put out would work. I only had 1 ad set up, so it wasn't enough. Something you think might work in ad copy doesn't always work. I got advice from a marketing expert: "the things you think might work won't always work, so you need to split test your ads. 5-10 ads to see which ones start working." Out of the 10 I set up, 2 that I didn't think would work ended up working best to start generating leads.

I started to get leads landing on my promotion page, but I wasn't able to book any appointments. I didn't test the links before launching, so I had to go back and figure out what the issue is, why my leads weren't converting to the calendar. Turns out, I was sending them to a calendar that had a totally different service than what they were opting in for. I was sending them to the wrong scheduler. Once I figured out what was happening, I started to convert leads. If I'd tested before, I would've been able to convert more leads.

After that, I had 50 leads, and 10 book, which was better than before, but it was still a really low conversion rate compared to previous campaigns. I thought, "Why is my conversion so low? The booking page is good." Come to find out, the form had different questions than went with the service. The questions weren't relating to the service I was providing. The questions weren't relating to their pains. So they weren't booking. Once I adjusted the questions to that, I started getting an 80-90% conversion rate.

Now you have people that are booked. They need to show up in order to close them. Say your confirmation system is down or not working properly, they aren't getting the automated reminder messages or confirming. People need to be reminded.

In the campaign where I made all those mistakes, I made yet another one: People were in the wrong campaign of automated reminders. I wondered why my show up rate was so low. Come to find out, my automated messages were not about x they were about y, so I had to make changes to get higher show-up rates. [higher show-up rate is the higher close rate]

See how many times in the funnel there was a mistake and a missed opportunity! I wasted a lot of time, and lost out on some opportunities by not taking the time to test my campaign. Build it into your system to always, always, test and re-test before launching.

After I made so many mistakes with that one campaign, I looked back through my process and found the simplest, most effective change I could make: checking my links before launching. Now, I could've just sat around and stressed out about why my campaign wasn't doing well. I've done that before, too, before I learned how to have a plan to evaluate how well my campaigns and business are doing.

As you integrate all these new skills and techniques into how you run your business, you will make mistakes. Some of those mistakes you can look to books or experts or colleagues for an answer. Some require patience and a willingness to comb through your steps with an objective eye so that you'll be able to notice where your simplest, most effective change is.

In terms of delegating automated funnels, if you have staff, you want to hand off building the funnels as much as possible. If you work for yourself, take a look at your big picture and see if it is worth investing in hiring someone to help. As the visionary, it's your job to create the idea for the campaign (or have the final say on the best idea), make sure it proceeds in a timely manner, and make sure it gets objectively evaluated for what worked and what didn't so the next campaign can incorporate those improvements. Actually building the funnels and texts and emails is best handed off, as it is time-consuming and not the most ideal investment of your time.

Maybe you can't hand it off. Maybe you want to get good at it yourself before handing off so you know what you're looking for in others' work. Maybe there is someone on your staff who already knows more about building these sorts of automated emails and texts than you do.

Step back, take a look at your big picture and develop your system for getting the work of building the funnel done right.

AUTOMATE YOUR PROCESSES

Review: Healthy Body = Healthy Business

If you aren't healthy, your business is going to feel it. Take a moment to sit quietly with your eyes closed. Check in with how your body feels. Ask, and listen. Does your body feel rested, nourished, energized, at peace? Does it feel frazzled, exhausted, sluggish, or weak? Or do different parts of your body feel different? Maybe your whole body except your neck and toes feels great. Every body is unique. Take a moment to sit and ask your body how it is doing, and listen to how it feels.

Now, sit with that information. What is it telling you?

Now, sit with how your mind takes in that information. Does listening to your body make your mind feel stressed, overwhelmed, guilty, ashamed, or exhausted? Why is that? Where is that coming from?

Now, how often do you actually step back and listen to your body? How well have you built up your habits around taking care of your body? How can you start to get that back on track? Do you need to repeat the first month? No shame if you do, just own it and start to tackle whatever it is that you know you need to do to up your healthy body game. Without a healthy body, you are not going to have a healthy business. Let alone be able to truly enjoy your work and your success.

Self-reflection & an open mind

When working with other business owners, I find time and again that the biggest impediment to the acceleration of their business is a lack of an open mind. It's easy to let the stress and hustle of the day-to-day of running a small business justify closing your mind to new ideas. New ideas take work! It can feel like it simplifies things to close down and resist new ideas. But in the long run, it really only makes things harder. Time and again, I've seen people lose out on opportunities and easefulness by rejecting new ideas just because they are new and uncomfortable at first.

Take a moment and flip back to your notes from the first 5 months. How has your mind changed in the course of working through this material? How have your self-reflection skills improved, and what have the effects been? What ideas, concepts, or principles were you initially resistant to, and what happened as a result of overcoming your resistance?

How can you keep these two powerful principles of self-reflection and an open mind alive and well? How have they become an integral part of running your business?

Inspiring staff

Everyone needs a personal touch--that sense of connection with their boss and coworkers. That sense of connection is the lifeblood of a business, and it's your job to keep the pulse healthy.

Everyone needs their own time with their employer. Take 15-20 min each week to connect with each employee, how they're doing where their mind is at. Then they appreciate you more and treat their job as 'more than a job.' If this is still a struggle for you, don't sweat it—but don't avoid it. Flip back to chapter 3 and see if there is anything you can implement or take away to help you develop your ability to build rapport with staff. Take a few moments to reflect on the journey with your staff rapport-building skills over the past 7 months.

Team meetings and staff trainings are just as important when it comes to the healthy pulse of your staff. Staff meetings and trainings should never be just about the business. There are always 2 goals, equally important and mutually reinforcing. The first goal is training them and make them better in terms of a specific goal, skill, outcome, etc. The second goal is that natural sense of team camaraderie. Remember, camaraderie isn't just about sharing jokes and being light-hearted. Team camaraderie also means people feel safe to express their frustrations and stresses, and know how to do it in a respectful way within the boundaries of how your group operates. Take a moment to reflect on if your staff could improve how they share what frustrates them with each other and you.

The personal touch

Who you are as a person is the heart and soul of the individuality and unique amazingness that is your company. You want that personal, ineffable thing to infuse everything your company does. You don't want it to 'get lost' in the midst of all these changes and transitions in how you do business.

First, trust yourself and the impetus that got you here in the first place. That personal touch will continue to infuse everything your company does, so long as you care and are dedicated to your company. Small business owners love what they do because they love that sense of the personal, local, unique that is a small business. Their customers love their business for that same reason.

Review month 4, week 2 and month 9, week 1 about authenticity, branding and connecting with honesty.

If you like, flip through the material on building automated campaigns and closing the sale.

Now, take a moment to think about what it is that is your unique personal touch that infuses the whole business no matter what. Maybe it is your cool logo. Maybe it is that you love to have FB private chats with customers and ask them questions. Maybe it is the creative names for your services/goods. Maybe it is the new blog you've launched, or the way you sign off on emails or texts. Maybe it's the unique way you train and connect with your staff.

Take a step back and look at the big picture of your company. Where is the pulse of your personal touch the most energizing to you?

Find a way to capture that energy so it shows up when you are designing your future marketing campaigns, social media posts, and new pages for your website. Maybe it's a file of screenshots of messages with happy customers, maybe it's a picture of you and your staff. Find that symbol that speaks strongly to the pulse of the personal in your business. Develop a creative way to incorporate it into your brainstorming time.

Minimizing effort/maximizing the value of your time

For the past 15 years, I've been running my business. It's been the same routine that helps me stay focused. First thing I do is work out. While I'm working out, I'm planning my day. I was able to plan my whole entire day, plan meetings, follow-up, confirm, book calls, set up to-do list for day, and because I worked out, it gave me the adrenaline and energy for the entire day.

About 5 years ago I decided to make a change. I'd been running my business for 10 years, and started feeling tired of it. Even though my business was successful, I wanted to change my routine, do something different. At same time I was really happy with where I was in life: waking up, training physically, then going to work, I had a really good lifestyle.

But, I decided that feeling of stagnation meant I needed a complete overhaul. Making those changes frustrated me even more! I had to rebuild a whole entire system, a whole entire routine. That took WAY more energy and effort than I realized, and in making the effort, I realized I made a mistake about how I chose to address my inner feeling of stagnation. I didn't have to change the whole system, I just needed a few tweaks.

So I went back to my old routine that I was happy with. Major changes in your life actually could break you down. If you're making major changes gradually implement them instead of changing whole routine with one shot.

How to Keep tomorrow in mind: Long-term Decisions & Software

Change is inevitable, and it is human nature to struggle with it. We resist it, we run from it, and in some cases we cling to it or act foolishly in terms of organizing change into our lives or in dealing with the unexpected.

When it comes to running a business, you have to own your biases and how you react or prepare for change.

Especially when it comes to your software.

I'm currently using a software that has all of my leads and clients, and I've set up a lot of different automations. I'm very hesitant on changing software, which I have to do because this software is 10 years out of date and not really meeting my needs any more. I don't want to change, it's going to be a lot of work, but I will do it. I already know it's going to take time to learn the new software, migrate all my automations to the new software (which the other software providers won't want to help with). My software is a good software, but they are outdated and not up-to-speed with the times. They were 5 years ahead, now they are a few years behind.

So, my advice is buy the software that's ahead of the game, use it until it's a few years out of date, then give yourself plenty of time to make the migration. It's going to be a pain. It's going to take a lot of work. But it is way better than cruising along with software that doesn't really meet your needs. Keep tomorrow in mind by riding that wave of change and advancement in tech without crashing out.

Some businesses don't even have CRM. It's stopping their growth. A software that can actually manage their businesses better. Trust me, I know how frustrating and challenging and hard to find the time and really learn the program and build the automations it all is. It's worth it.

Software is a tool for growth. So, how is that process of finding that right set of software for you going? You ready to make a commitment to a software and learn to maximize the use of its programs?

Personal Honesty & Reflection when it comes to software use

I've signed up for a free software program before, all excited and carried away by the glitz and glam of its features.

And then never used it again.

And I've done it and used it a few times and then never used it again.

I've also used a program for just a couple features and never really learned how to make the most of everything that program has to offer.

It's easy to make all those mistakes. Hard to learn to overcome them. Like I've said time and again, make changes slowly, but consistently.

Be honest—is some part of your mind still thinking that it's not really worth it to invest in purchasing/adopting and integrating software programs to help you automate?

Think of it this way.

Everybody has the same main complaint: not enough customers.

How are you going to get more customers if you don't extend your reach and get more eyeballs on what you have to offer?

Why wouldn't you extend your reach in the way that is the easiest and most efficient use of your time?

Finding good software that does everything we've covered IS the easiest and most efficient use of your time. Sure, it is a pain to migrate and learn new features and tools. But once you've done it, the pain is over. When you're using outdated software or software that doesn't really meet your needs, you feel that pain every day.

Go forth and master that software.

You've got the skills, tools, and resources. Trust yourself. Trust the experiment to get you where you need to go.

MONTH TWELVE
YOUR PRIORITIES DIRECT YOUR BUSINESS

This section circles back around to one of the main themes: you are the visionary. If you don't tend to your time, your goals, and your creative strategy for achieving those goals, then you don't have clear priorities. And when you don't have clear priorities, your time gets wasted, you either don't set goals, or you don't end up moving toward accomplishing those goals.

For a small business owner, it's best to think about prioritizing along multiple lines of effort. By this I mean prioritizing your projects at the daily, weekly, monthly, and yearly levels. All your priorities should align with one another toward your long-term vision for the company. A lot of these chapters have been about introducing new priorities for your business and how to integrate them into operations. Your yearly priorities set your monthly ones, and so on down the line. Some priorities are maintenance (keeping website updated, booking, etc), and some are expansionary in nature (marketing, learning new skills, delegating, etc).

It takes some trial and error to learn how to navigate setting and sticking to priorities that interlink like this, but as you master the skill, you will free up your time and become more efficient across the board. In many ways, we've been practicing this all along, this is about tying up the loose ends and owning mastery.

Whether your priorities are at the daily, monthly, yearly level, it all comes down to making a target list. For example, with my company, if we are planning for the whole year we start with setting a measurable goal for the entire company (i.e., 100 new regular clients in 1 year). Then, we divide that out into the priorities for the different teams, and within that, for each individual within that team. Priorities are a blend of personal development and skill-building and measurable accomplishments for the company.

I often like to take time to brainstorm and list out all of my goals, then narrow them down into how many I think can be accomplished in one year. (and remember, it takes some trial and error to get really good at estimating time on projects).

Then, once I have my list, say I have 10 goals for the upcoming year. The most important goal has to be met first. Then the second most important goal. Prioritize by importance. Also, take note of how much time and money each goal takes, how many other people have to be involved, etc.

Same thing goes for the day-to-day. When you wake up in the morning, start with a list of the things you need to take care of. What is the most important thing that needs to be taken care of first?

We all know about making lists. What we don't always have a grip on is how to deal successfully with that list. It's like human nature for a person to do the least important things first because they are the easiest to take care of. And they leave the things that are most important to last. And what ends up happening is the most important things don't get done.

There is an app called 'commit to 3'. The app makes you set the key elements for the day, 3 most important things that you have to do for that day. It shoots you notifications that you use to complete those tasks & send reminders for your commitment for the day. A software program like that might be a great way for you to start to turn your ability to prioritize around, if it's a struggle for you like it is for so many.

Doing the most important things first makes you more productive in your business.

So, as the leader of your business, perhaps the most essential skill you must have is creating your priorities and making sure to do the most important things first. And, if you have staff, teach them the same.

You are fighting your own human nature to switch to creating a list of priorities and taking care of the biggest priorities first, and you might have to undo some bad habits and ways of thinking, but plain and simple, if you aren't prioritizing and sticking to it, your goals won't get accomplished.

Take a moment to reflect on your habits as a prioritizer. What does your current normal look like when it comes to setting and following through on prioritizing at the daily, weekly, and yearly level? How did you learn these habits? What major lessons has life taught you about prioritizing and following through?

MAKING A MAP

A great strategy for understanding your priorities in any given project is to make a map. You can be as creative as you want with your visualizations. Some people like to use Excel, some like markers and whiteboards.

I had this amazing idea for a marketing campaign. I made artwork for it for fliers, postcards, and doorhangers. I built a landing page for the funnel so people could opt in and go through my funnel and the entire sales process. It took me a couple weeks to get it all done and printed. I didn't do the most important thing, which was find people to distribute my fliers, postcards, and doorhangers. I didn't take ads out to find people to distribute my artwork. The fliers had a date on them. Since I didn't take the time to schedule people to deliver them, the artwork got stale and I lost money on the campaign because nobody distributed my ads. Nobody put out the postcards, doorhangers, gave out the business cards. Since this campaign had an expiration date, I had to throw the whole project out or recreate it because it was time sensitive.

I should have found distributors first, then made a deadline for when artwork was prepared by. Then if I'd had a deadline, I'd've met it. So people would be there ready to distribute, by the time people got to it, it was already too late, time to start a new campaign.

Your first time through a new campaign or way of doing things, you aren't always going to get your priorities right. That's okay! Learn from my mistakes, learn from your mistakes, keep improving at prioritizing.

When starting a new goal or project, make a list, a map for yourself of what you need to take care of. Then, figure out what in that map should get done first. Then once you understand that, you'll understand what happens second, what requires more time, where is the urgency, so that way what does take a bunch of time will get executed.

It all depends on timing how far ahead to plan. So for seasonal changes, start at least a month ahead, not a week ahead. Let's say you're in the fitness industry, you're not going to want to advertise fitness for summer during summer, you're going to do need to start during spring. (hey, remember using your calendar to block time? Set up automated yearly reminders a month out for all your planning-your-priorities meetings for big, regular projects).

Marketing campaigns are one of your biggest priorities, and you are going to need to get really good at keeping it a priority, and creating good maps for your campaigns. There is no cut and dry method, it all depends on the size of the project and type of campaign. For example, Black Friday, companies advertise it way ahead, like a month before. They tell you the day is going to be a big deal and what items are going to be on sale on that specific website. Tons of companies participate in Black Friday so everyone is competing for those eyeballs, so everyone needs to create specific specials and deals for when people come to them and not go to anybody else. Maybe they need to create something special just for getting people to land on the page—breaking even or losing money on the specific item but making money in the long run because people went to the website and purchased other items.

Here is a basic map for you to use for marketing campaigns. Over time as you get reps designing and launching campaigns, your map will start to be more intuitive and unique to you.

- o   Brainstorm
- o   Create
- o   Monitor & Adjust
- o   Evaluate & Incorporate Changes
- o   Brainstorm and create offer
- o   Brainstorm machine gun marketing tactics
- o   Create written copy
- o   Create artwork

o Print ads
o Design funnel
o Create website/social media pages, posts, and ads for funnel
o Test funnel
o Distribute print ads
o Monitor and assess campaign

As you practice this map, and make it your own, you'll start to get a feel for how much time each part takes, and when and how each part should be done. For the creative, generative and reflective/troubleshooting aspects, you'll want to keep building on the techniques we've been practicing regarding your individual methods for bringing your creativity out.

Own Your Priorities

You've graduated: I don't want to be in charge of delegating tasks and skills for you to build, I want you to set your own priorities, both with keeping up with the reading and insights of this book, and with you learning how you need to apply the concepts.

So in keeping track of your yearly, daily, and weekly goals, you need to use your calendar. You need to use the seasonal rhythms that your business fits with, to include local and national ones. You need to set aside time to figure out what those rhythms are, how they're changing, and how you can fit your marketing campaigns to match up.

Most importantly, you need to make developing and running marketing campaigns one of your top 3 priorities. Every day, one of your top tasks should probably include something to do with marketing. I meet a lot of small business owners who are very uncomfortable with marketing in general, and the new ways marketing happens now in particular. I always say, people are incredibly busy. The world moves faster and faster. If you don't use techniques proven to help people remember that they want to solve the problems that your business can solve, then it's not going to happen. Marketing at its best is a win-win-win. But you have to be the one keeping it as a main priority for your business.

Having connections plays a big role in business

Along with having that map for your projects, another essential priority for every small business is that network of connections. I know, I know, it's easy to be cynical and lose sight of boundaries between personal/professional, or have some other reason for not taking a deliberate, intentional approach to maintaining and expanding your network. If you have integrity, your network will have integrity. Think about it, we all naturally have a network as part of being human. Maybe interacting with people isn't your favorite cup of tea—and you don't have to follow a rote model for connection building, it should spring from who you are as a unique person—but it is a good rule of thumb to have as a consistent priority building and maintaining your network.

Again, don't treat it as this mechanical thing where you lose sight of your humanity and other people's humanity. That's not what I'm saying. I'm saying as a small business owner in an information-laden and fast-paced world, we need our networks as much, if not more, than any other time in human history.

Let me share a story that illustrates the power of connections.

The son of one of my long-time clients, a 17-year-old I had known since he was 2, started selling drugs and got caught.

He wasn't a big-time dealer, just selling a little bit, thought it was an easy way to make money. Normally, police get in with the small-fry to try to catch the bigger fish, but this time, the police officer bought a little bit, then made the arrest, and he went to jail.

His mother contacted me, "Alex, big problem, my son just got arrested. For selling drugs." I was shocked. He's been a good kid, good worker, caring. I watched him grow up. Even through my shock, I responded without hesitation, "What do you need help with?" "I need a good lawyer." So I went to my networking group, and shared that I needed a criminal lawyer. Within an hour, we had 20 hits of people tagging their attorneys.

I sent her a couple, she called one. This attorney was good. He was able to 1, get kid out of jail. 2, able to have kid do community service and charges dropped because he's young and this was his first offense.

This story could have gone a different direction.

They could have hired a different person, or taken a long time, money, and aggravation. The kid could have stayed in jail a lot longer.

without a good attorney, those charges would have stayed on his record which would have severely, negatively affected the rest of his life. Employers do not like to see such behavior on job applicant's histories.

My student who is a police officer, go to police and speak to arresting officer and let them know that this kid is a good kid, and this is his first offense. To lighten up the pressure.

'When you have a strong network, shit gets easier.'

MAKING MISTAKES

Learning from mistakes is an essential part of the process. Hopefully, the young man from the last section will take full advantage of his opportunity to learn from his mistake, and enter adulthood with fresh perspective on his decision-making.

Before I share another story on mistakes, one last delegation of tasks. I'm always listening to podcasts, always taking classes, always talking to experts and my staff to learn from them. I have now taken so many classes (and made so many mistakes!) on social media and marketing that I'm able to start my own company on social media marketing. I am still taking classes and still feel that I have a lot to learn, but after over a decade of learning, I'm now able to translate that knowledge, not just into profit for my business, but also into a profitable new business! So, one last time, look at your week and see when and how and where you can make learning more of a priority for yourself.

Now, the last story.

A good friend of mine, Steven, who is now a high-level executive in a very successful company, did not always see learning as a priority. In New York, as part of completing high school, you have to take these final examinations called Regent's Exams. Well, Steven didn't like math so much that he sent somebody else to take the Regents Examination. The exam is proctored by a randomly chosen teacher from the area, so I'm sure my very confident friend thought it would be all too easy to get away with his scheme. But, in a quirk of fate, that day his teacher was the proctor. Some other teenager, Joe, walks in to take the test under Steven's name, and the teacher is looking at Joe going, you're not Steven, who are you? Joe—as the teacher is talking, trying to process what's going on—grabs his bag, pushes the teacher and starts running.

In the middle of the hallway there were these doors that swing both ways, he pushes the door open, runs out, sees the security guard by the stairs, says please help. The security guard grabs proctor while Joe runs outside into the snow. He climbs over the school fence, then runs into somebody else's backyard and hides for 20 minutes, in the snow, while it's snowing. Security guards and teachers search for him. After waiting out the search parties, he comes out to car where Steven is waiting for him.

Steven was expelled from school.

He wasn't a bad student... just was terrible at math. He thought he could get away with not doing all the work, and ended up having to take night school to finish his diploma.

I love sharing this story, because Steven is now very successful. It was a big mistake. He was trying to avoid things he didn't want to learn. I think Steven was really lucky that he didn't get away with it, it forced him to have to work harder to reach the finish line, and it taught him that mistakes are just part of being human, part of the process.

I see people making that kind of mistake of avoiding learning all the time, it's human nature. I wanted to close with this story to remind you to stay the course on being a lifelong learner, and to not let your mistakes be a reason to give up on your business.

If you keep owning your mistakes as part of your personal priorities as you build marketing campaigns, launch new products, etc, your business will continue to grow and succeed, but more than that, you will truly be able to enjoy your life and the fruits of your success.

It's okay to make mistakes, but don't make the same mistakes. Also, you don't want to just learn from your mistakes, but overcome them. Steven went on to become very successful. If you make a mistake with your website, don't just learn how to fix the landing page, overcome your whole struggle with websites.

When I started my company 10 years ago, like my friend when he was in high school, I didn't realize how important it was to educate yourself. The things that I educated myself on were the things that interested me. That's how I was in high school and college, I worked really hard in the subjects I loved and at the martial arts studio, but if it wasn't interesting, I didn't put much effort in. But after taking a learner mindset as a business owner, that old hatred of history and geography has gone away. I realized I do have an interest in learning about maps and history. I'm close to 40, and still don't know so much! But the more I commit to learning, the more curious and interested in learning about things I am. And somehow, it all always feeds back into living a better, more fulfilling life, and running a more successful business.

AT THE END OF THE DAY, ONLY YOU CAN DECIDE WHAT'S BEST FOR YOUR BIZ

Arnold Schwarzenegger has 6 rules for success. One of them is, you need to bend the rules to be successful. You can't always play by the book.

Now, in marketing there's a lot of things you're not allowed to do. Soliciting. One of the rules I have to bend to promote myself, my business. One rule is, no fliers in mailboxes because they are post office property. You're also not allowed to put fliers on cars, poles, transformer boxes, etc. In order to promote my business, I bend those rules, I have to let the public know that my business exists. So I place postcards and ads on cars and in mailboxes.

It did help me accelerate my growth. I did break the rules. I was expecting a summons, I was prepared to pay a ticket. Sometimes you don't get caught. It's breaking the rules, but at the same time, I decided it was necessary to accelerate the growth and get more eyeballs on my business.

If you're going to bend the rules, you must be willing to accept the consequences. When we market this way, we are ready for the consequences. Any time someone calls about a flier stuck on the windshield, my well-trained staff will say, "We're very sorry about that, please come by our studio and one of our staff will remove it." We have all the supplies on hand, and act promptly and respectfully when they come by. Out of the thousands of fliers we've sent out this way, only a few people have called with this complaint. It is a risk I was willing to take as part of bending the rule in order to do what I thought was best for getting the word out about my business.

KEEP FEEDING YOUR MIND

Exercising shapes your body and motivates you to perform, but the mind also needs to be fed with education and motivation.

Feeding the mind in our society requires dedication and discipline. There's always a lot going on, and to gain traction and long-term 'nourishment' of your mind, you have to make a commitment to it, just like with diet and exercise. And, once you build the habit, it'll be easier, and you'll miss it when you go a few days without it. Time in the car or while working out is a great way to keep feeding your mind. Remember to keep it a blend of stuff relevant to running a small business as well as stuff that piques your curiosity.

Your mind also gets fed by recharging. You need to recharge every day, not just with a good diet, but with spending time with loved ones, and doing things that aren't related to work. I see so many small business owners burn out, because they can't turn it off, they're always working, or thinking and stressing about work. Nobody can live like that for very long. No business can sustain with a leader who lives like that. Use your calendar and your new skills of self-reflection and planning and delegating to recharge and rest.

I also make sure to take at least 2 vacations every year. I love that time because I get to be with my family with no plans and nowhere to be other than where we want to go. I even love the fights and disagreements, because we are all together. My wife and I bring books and podcasts that we listen to on the flight and when we're relaxing by the pool or beach, just because we love to learn. I always come back from my trips full of inspiration, motivation, and new ideas. When you have time on your hands not related to work, you come up with new content, fresh ideas. You refresh your spirit, step away and gain new perspective and new fuel for your creativity and drive.

While everyone stays motivated by a healthy lifestyle, feeding the mind, and rest, we all have our unique things that keep us motivated. How you stay motivated is unique to you. Maybe its prayer or meditation. Maybe its driving to work listening to tunes that pump you up. Maybe it's having a clear goal and steps for getting there. Maybe it's coming home at the end of every day and laughing and venting about how the day went.

Motivation, like diet, exercise, and rest, is best as a preventative measure. When you take a little time every day to connect to your inner drive, then when shit hits the fan, you'll be resilient, you won't get knocked completely out of balance. Motivation powers you through the mistakes and the hard times.

Remember, I've made almost every mistake when it comes to marketing in this new era of business that could be made. I've had to shut down a store.

I really believed that I would be able to open up a second location. I bought out somebody else's standing business. I took over the business, it started to slowly grow. One of my weaknesses was that I couldn't manage my time between two businesses. Whichever one I wasn't putting time into, was going down in terms of profitability. I didn't have a strong enough system, and maybe the right people in place to run that new location.

At the same time, staff in both locations would revert to their old ways instead of following my lead on their assigned tasks.

I was losing a lot of money, yet I was convinced I'd be able to do it, I kept pushing it and pushing it. Finally, I decided to sell the location. The company that took over also weren't successful, they sold after 3 years. I bought it back.

I thought, okay this time I'm really going to focus on this business. This whole time, I didn't realize that the location was in the wrong area, it was a neighborhood full of people who can't afford the services I was providing. I went into the red for another year. Finally, I decided, enough was enough, let bygones be bygones, and I let things go, I sold the store for the final time.

After that, things starting falling into place. I spent a lot of time losing money and stressing out, putting all my time in to absolutely no avail. It's okay to let go. One door closes, 10 others will open, and you will have time for those 10 other opportunities.

None of your mistakes guarantee failure. Not at all. So stay strong, because you've got a beautiful vision for your company, and your community deserves to experience it.

For workbooks and workshops of the book, join the Small Business Online University:

Small Business Online University,
www.SmallBusinessOnlineUniversity.com

You Can Also Join My Small Business Networking Group,
https://www.facebook.com/groups/SmallBusinessProfitArsenal/

For Business Coaching, Educational Speaking, and Consultations,
www.AlexDavydov.com

Need help with social media marketing?
www.SocialChaosMarketing.com

Printed in the United States
By Bookmasters